25 FREIGHT CAR PROJECTS

Edited by Randy Rehberg

KALMBACH BOOKS

WAUKESHA, WI

Kalmbach Books
21027 Crossroads Circle
Waukesha, Wisconsin 53186
www.Kalmbach.com/Books

Published in 2016
20 19 18 17 16   1 2 3 4 5

Manufactured in China

ISBN: 978-1-62700-278-3
EISBN: 978-1-62700-279-0

Editor: Randy Rehberg
Book Design: Tom Ford

Unless noted, photographs were taken by the authors.

Library of Congress Control Number: 2015920081

Contents

Weathering with artist's pastels

By Tony Koester

1

The essential ingredients are a freight car with a dead-flat finish, PanPastel weathering media, and foam applicators. Left to right: 780.3 Raw Umber Tint, 820.1 Neutral Grey Dark, 740.3 Burnt Sienna Shade, and 380.3 Red Iron Oxide Shade.

So much to do, so little time to do it, especially where leisure-time activities are concerned. I am therefore always looking for shortcuts and efficiencies where my modeling projects are concerned.

Several years ago, Rob Manley gave a presentation at the Railroad Prototype Modelers (rpm.org) meet in Naperville, Ill., about a new weathering material he had come across. It's marketed as PanPastels (panpastel.com) by Colorfin of Kutztown, Pa.

PanPastels were created as a replacement for pastel chalks used by artists.

Modelers have used pastel chalks and powders as a weathering (aging) medium for years, but PanPastels are different.

They come in round plastic containers like the ones makeup are sold in, but they are not makeup in disguise. They're also not simply pastel chalks in another form, either, as they have a binder that makes them adhere well to paper and other matte surfaces.

Inspired by Rob's demonstration, I ordered a range of colors from black to white and various earth colors that could be used to represent grime, soot, rust, and dust. PanPastels are now sold in weathering kits with a range of colors, which eases the task of selecting appropriate colors, **1**.

I have also used PanPastels—sky blues, grays, and white for clouds and various greens for foliage—to blend the joints between unrelated digital backdrop photos.

What follows is a primer and is not intended to produce contest-winning models. Rather, my goal is to show you how easy—and fast!—it is to add visual variety to your rolling stock fleet while ensuring that every car doesn't look like it came out of the paint shop earlier today. Equally important, PanPastels can serve as a form of drybrushing to highlight details. There's virtually no risk—you can always wash off PanPastels and start over.

While focusing here on rolling stock, PanPastels work equally well on structures and locomotives (see "Weathering a steam locomotive in 7 minutes" in *Model Railroader* November 2013).

Think flat

The key to working with PanPastels is to apply them to an absolutely flat (matte) surface. They won't grip a surface that has a sheen or shine, but you don't want that on weathered cars anyway.

For shiny cars that are already assembled, I pop out the wheels and put masking tape over the couplers. I then spray them with Testor's Dullcote, usually from a "rattle can."

Before giving a car a dull overspray, I make sure I'm not adding a duplicate-number car to the roster. I create way-bills for every car using Microsoft Word and file them by car number so I can instantly spot a duplicate.

Accurail makes it easy to change car numbers by selling decal sheets with the background color matching the body color of their kits, **2**. There is no need to remove the numerals to be replaced.

My railroad's standard is metal wheels from InterMountain or NorthWest Short Line, which have a shiny surface. On modern cars with

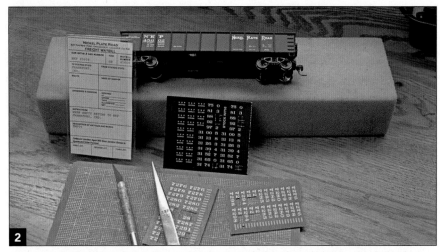

Accurail makes special opaque-background decals color-matched to their kits. You can therefore change the car number without removing the original digits.

Weathering metal wheels is as easy as wiping around the outer surface with the tip of a rail brown or grimy black weathering pen while holding the wheelset in your hand.

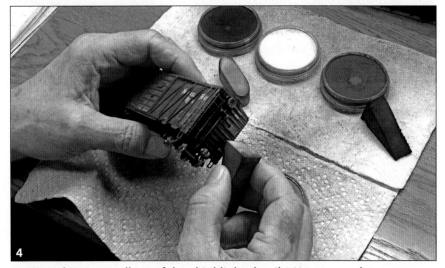

PanPastels are equally useful to highlight details. Use a complementary light color on a dark model (gray or charcoal on black, for example) and a darker color on a light-colored model.

These before-and-after photos of Accurail gondolas and open hoppers show how an in-service look was achieved with PanPastels in only a few minutes. No fixative needs to be applied, and the weathering can be wiped or washed off if at first you don't succeed.

The fish-belly underframe on a wood boxcar was later replaced with a steel channel. This is easy to do on Accurail single-sheathed boxcars with strips of .030" x .125" styrene.

roller-bearing trucks, wheels often have a rusty appearance. But cars in the steam era usually had plain (friction) bearings, and the oil from the journal boxes typically leaked onto the wheels. I therefore use a dark brown or grimy black color, which is easy to apply by wiping the surface of the wheel (but not the axle point, tread, or flange) with a felt-tip weathering pen, **3**. Rail brown or grimy black is a good choice.

I also use Kadee couplers, and the copper-colored knuckle spring needs to be toned down, which I do with a touch of grungy black paint. A bit of rust on the coupler itself is also appropriate.

The drybrushing effect
Before continuing, remember that you're not only trying to suggest a car's age and usage but also highlighting its factory-added details.

When using paint, do this by dipping the tip of a stiff-bristled brush into a light color, scrubbing off most of the paint, and then wiping the almost-dry bristles across any details that you want to be more visible. You do the

same thing with PanPastels. In fact, most of what you're doing is highlighting details, **4**. Once you have done that, you can add some aging and heavy-usage effects.

Getting started with a gon
Let's start with an easy-to-build plastic kit. Accurail gondolas and hoppers come with a dead-flat finish, which is ideal for weathering with PanPastels, **5**. Its 40-foot USRA gondola is among the finest plastic kits on the market, as fragile parts such as the steps and brake lines are molded in flexible engineering plastic. (Use cyanoacrylate adhesive, or CA, to attach the brake lines to the gondola's underframe; the steps snap in place.)

An inky black gon doesn't look the part, so the first step is to wipe down the sides, ends, and interior with a charcoal color. I use PanPastel no. 820.1 called Neutral Grey Extra Dark. Other handy hues are 800.5 Black, 820.3 Neutral Grey Shade, 100.5 Titanium White, and 380.1 Red Iron Oxide Extra Dark. Colorfin sells foam applicators similar to those used to apply makeup, but they're actually quite a bit firmer. I find the wedge-shape applicator especially handy—I use the pointed tip to get into the interior corners—but I recommend buying a variety.

I then lightly coat the same applicator with a rust color (no. 380.3, Red Iron Oxide Shade). I wipe this over the ribs and then on all interior surfaces. I use the same grungy applicator to apply a light dust color along the bottom edges of the sides and ends and on the truck sideframes.

About two minutes later, I'm done.

Weathering steel hoppers
Weathering a steel hopper is essentially the same exercise. The interior surface of the slope sheets may have a shiny metallic surface after a coal or aggregate load has been dumped, but that won't last for long.

In the winter, the coal may freeze in the car. Local coal dealers don't have heating sheds like those used at utility plants, so a small bonfire is often built under the hopper bays. The heating causes the paint to blister off, leaving a triangular rusty area delineating the open area between the hopper bays.

Single-sheathed boxcars

Wood boxcars often had vertically planked wood sides covering wood or metal truss members, and the interiors were also lined with wood. These were called *double-sheathed* boxcars.

In some cases, the exterior siding was deemed superfluous, and the resulting cars were called *single-sheathed* (not outside-braced). Modern steel cars with the vertical support members exposed are called *exterior-post* boxcars.

The Accurail single-sheathed boxcar has been both praised and criticized for the obvious grain evident in the wood sides. It's difficult to replicate some details to scale and still have them evident to viewers, so I like the texture that the molded-in grain provides. HO scale grain would be invisible.

The Accurail kit represents an as-built car with the deep fish-belly underframe. Many, if not all, of these cars were rebuilt with steel-channel underframes. This is easy to simulate by discarding the molded fish-belly parts and inserting six identical .030" x .125" strips of styrene (Evergreen no. 146) into the molded-in slots, **6**. Cut and fit one strip as a master and then use it as a pattern to cut the rest.

Most hobby shops carry Canopy Cement, which looks like regular white glue but is a very different product. As its name implies, it dries clear, hence its use for attaching canopies to model aircraft. But its ability to bond various types of materials to each other creates myriad applications for a model railroader, including attaching steel weights to the plastic floor. It contains no solvents that over time will attack the plastic and cause it to curl. Unlike CA, it retains a degree of resilience.

In the steam era, everything was covered with soot from coal- or oil-burning steam locomotives, so let's start by wiping down the car sides, ends, and finally the roof with a charcoal color, **7** and **8**. The paint often wore off the running boards (not roofwalks), so I wipe them with a medium to light gray. As with the gondola and hopper, I

7 The right half of the steel double-door boxcar has had a light gray wash applied. I then added charcoal grime streaks at the end of the door track, and a dust color along the carbody bottom and on truck sideframes.

8 A single-sheathed boxcar like CN 500795 quickly shows soot and road grime in the wood grain and around the steel truss members. The usual gray, charcoal, and rust colors quickly add an appropriate amount of weathering.

lightly coat the lower car side and truck sideframes with a dust color.

The final step

The last thing to do after weathering a car with PanPastels is—nothing! Unlike weathering chalks, PanPastels usually don't need to have a clear coat applied to seal them. They bond well to the texture of the flat surface.

If a model will be handled a great deal, you could apply a seal coat. But normal handling of cars and even locomotives, which happens when I restage the railroad between operating sessions

and rearrange the order of cars in trains, does not require a clear coat.

Onward!

Now that you're familiar with the time-saving aspects of PanPastels, you can try them on locomotives and structures. For example, I use a rattle can to spray-paint brick buildings with an oxide primer color and then wipe the entire surface with a similar PanPastel color. This ensures a dead-flat finish, which is exactly what you want for a brick wall, and it makes it easy to have some variation in the color.

Patching freight cars with paint pens

By James McNab

1

The HO scale IAIS Grimes Line layout required a large number of freight cars to be re-stenciled for new owners. Using paint pens prevented the time-consuming and often tedious process of masking and painting with an airbrush.

One of the hallmarks of modeling a modern-era railroad is the presence of patched-out freight cars. These railroad hand-me-downs are a common sight on Class I, regional, and shortline railroads. Rolling stock built and purchased for one line often finds new life in the service of another railroad. This procedure also allows smaller and less prosperous lines to quickly and easily build a full roster.

Traditionally, modelers have covered factory-printed reporting marks with some combination of paint and decal film. This usually involves the tedious process of masking the area for painting, whether with an airbrush or by hand. It may be too much work to invest in if you have a small roster, or it might take too much time if you have a large roster. Depending on the number of cars you have to patch, this process may not be worth the outcome. Being able to quickly and easily reproduce each car, patched-out and ready for its new home, makes for a great model railroad.

My Iowa Interstate Grimes Industrial Track layout is firmly set in the modern era, **1**. The reporting marks on

2

When freight cars change ownership, the reporting marks need to be changed to reflect the new owner. The factory-painted reporting marks on this SNCT boxcar is covered with a simple swab of paint.

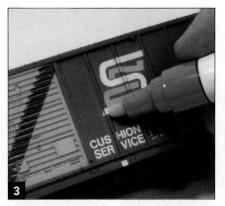

3

Some owners will patch and cover any marketing or promotional artwork on the sides of the cars. You are able to cover a large area in a short amount of time but make sure your strokes go in the same direction to minimize brushmarks.

4

Even the small reporting marks on the car ends can be quickly covered thanks to the variety of brush sizes available.

5

Patched freight cars offer the possibility of unique patterns and arrangements. The ragged edges of the patch reinforce the second-hand nature of the rolling stock.

6

Once the paint patch is dry, prepare the new car numbers. Reporting mark decals are available in various fonts, colors, and sizes to match a specific prototype.

most of my freight car fleet needed to be patched and re-stenciled for a new owner, **2**. I wanted to find a simple assembly line process that would let me complete the job quickly and efficiently, while still allowing me to model the specific cars I need for my prototype railroad.

Pens for the win

While on a trip to the local art supply store, I came across a display of paint pens. A paint pen (sometimes called a paint marker) is filled with oil-based paint and goes on similar to a permanent marker. Paint pens are inexpensive, readily available, and come in a large variety of colors.

Using prototype photos as a reference, I picked up several shades and colors to complete my entire car fleet. I tested the process on a cheap, blue boxcar to ensure it would work. The paint from the pen completely covered the factory-printed reporting marks with no bleedthrough from underneath.

Creating a reporting mark patch using a paint pen is considerably easier than using an airbrush. In the time it would take to set up an airbrush, mix, mask, and spray a single patch, I can patch-out several cars with a paint pen. The pen allows me to quickly apply a color to an area with maximum control and minimum effort, **3**. They also come in a variety of brush sizes and

shapes, allowing you to cover a variety of surfaces without having to mask the surrounding area, **4**.

Unlike patches painted by hand or with an airbrush, paint pens leave a more ragged appearance, which helps reinforce the second-hand nature of the rolling stock, **5**. Depending on the prototype you're modeling, you can create a series of cars with unique patterns and designs.

The patching process

Freight car reporting marks must be changed to the railroad that actually owns the car, since the new owner does not have the right to use the original railroad's initials. When a piece of

7 Letter by letter, new reporting marks are applied over the patched-out area. Larger rosters may require custom decals to speed up the process.

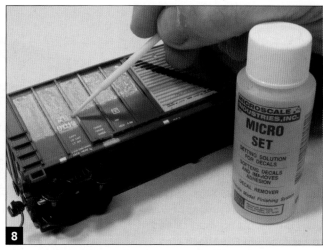

8 Once the decals are in place, apply Micro Set to permanently place the new reporting mark.

9 Weathering is done with a variety of powders, chalks, and inks on the rolling stock. Couplers and trucks receive a coat of grimy black.

10 Once the weathering process was complete, I sprayed Dullcote over the entire car and allowed it to dry.

rolling stock changes railroads, some new owners usually just paint over the reporting mark, leaving the rest of the car untouched. Others will cover any marketing or promotional artwork present on the side and, in essence, patch the entire car.

I started by covering over the reporting marks, making sure to leave the weight and capacity data untouched. I used only vertical strokes to minimize any brushmarks and best simulate the prototype patching process.

Using the same method, I covered promotional artwork on some cars. With several different types of paint pens available, I was able to cover a large area in a short amount of time. Again, I used prototype photos as my guide. The final result was a unique patchwork of paint on the sides of my car fleet.

Number by number

Once the paint had completely dried, I turned to re-stenciling the cars. Many manufacturers make ready-to-apply decals for numerous freight car reporting marks, including several modern era lines, **6**. By using Microscale's Condensed lettering set, I was able to match most of the prototype cars I was modeling, **7**. Several other fonts and typefaces are also available.

Number by number, I cut out and applied the new reporting mark decals to each freight car. I aligned each letter and number and let them settle before applying Micro Set setting solution, **8**. The process wasn't difficult or tedious,

especially for the low number of cars I had to re-stencil. Those of you with larger car fleets may consider having custom decals made to speed up the process. Either way, it takes only a small amount of time and effort to finish the decaling process.

With the decals in place, I began final detailing. Each car was weathered to best match its prototype, reflecting the hand-me-down appearance of a car that had spent years on the rails, **9**. Not every freight car was a rust bucket, since these cars are still responsible for generating revenue for their new owners. When I was satisfied with my weathering efforts, I sealed each car with Testor's Dullcote, installed Kadee scale couplers, and placed them into service on the railroad, **10**.

Upgrading a Burlington boxcar

By Jeff Wilson

1

A few basic details greatly improve the appearance of a stock Accurail boxcar kit, making it more closely match the prototype car.

I think Accurail's HO freight car kits rank among the best bargains in the hobby. Although many lack separate details, with most details molded in place, they generally have nice, accurate molding and sharp paint jobs. With a few added details, you can transform them into foreground models, **1**. You can use these techniques on almost any Accurail (or other) plastic car, regardless of road name, although I use a Burlington prototype.

The Accurail 40-foot steel boxcar follows the 1944 AAR design, which matches the Chicago, Burlington &

Quincy's late (class XM-32D) cars. In looking through prototype photos, I found a 1967 view of no. 61196, one of 2,250 cars built in 1953 (nos. 60000–62249).

In 1967, the prototype car was just a year removed from being rebuilt and repainted at the railroad's Havelock, Neb., shops, **2**. The car, originally painted mineral brown, received the Q's final Chinese red scheme, with a plain herald (the earlier version had a white stripe on either side of the herald). Since the Accurail model had the correct body style and paint scheme, with

2 This Chicago, Burlington & Quincy boxcar, built in 1953 and photographed in 1967, had been rebuilt just a year earlier. It received a new paint scheme and had its running board removed. *Hol Wagner*

3 Straight from the box, the Accurail car is not a bad model, but the brake gear is lacking, the brake wheel is heavy and crude, and the paint job needs some detail additions.

a number that fell in the same series, I decided to do a basic detail upgrade to better match the real thing, **3**.

Roof

When the car was rebuilt, running boards were being removed from existing cars (a process begun in 1966). For the model, the first job was to remove the running board. It's an injection-molded styrene piece, and can be simply pulled out of its mounting holes.

But then the holes must be filled. On some cars, the mounting pegs can be trimmed and used, provided the fit is tight enough. On this car, I used a piece of scrap sprue, sanded lightly so it fit tightly in each hole, **4**. Press the plugs in place and then add liquid

plastic cement from underneath. Let them sit overnight so the joint is solid.

Use a hobby knife to carefully shave off the supports for the lateral running boards at each corner as well as the end supports. Carve the plugs to match the existing roof texture, **5**. This is easier than it sounds, as the shapes of the various ridges help hide the fact that the plugs are separate. Use needle files to finish the job.

The model's original running board acted like a mask and left areas where the red paint didn't completely cover the black plastic. Find a color that matches the model's original as closely as possible (I used Modelflex caboose red). The quickest way to paint it is to airbrush it (mask the sides if you do

this), but you can also use a brush as I did here. Be aware that colors such as red don't cover well—it took several coats to do the trick, **6**.

Underbody

Accurail uses plastic friction pins to secure trucks and coupler box covers. I usually replace these with screws for a more secure fit. For the trucks, simply run a 2-56 tap in the existing mounting holes, **7**. For the couplers, start by trimming the existing pin off the box lid and drill a no. 43 clearance hole in its place. Drill out the existing mounting hole with a no. 50 bit and tap it 2-56. You can then use ³⁄₁₆"-long, 2-56 round-head screws to secure the lids, **8**.

You can use Accurail's own scale coupler or substitute a Kadee no. 5 (standard), 58 (scale, shown) coupler and spring, or any other coupler of your choice. I use manual uncoupling devices, so I usually cut off the steel uncoupling pins on my cars for better appearance—don't do this if you use magnetic uncouplers.

The Accurail car has only basic details on the underframe—brake cylinder, reservoir, and control valve, with no piping or rods. I'm not a stickler to have that detail modeled exactly. (As my friend Marty McGuirk says, "If you worry that much about underbody detail, you should probably focus on your trackwork a bit more.") However, I like to represent basic rods and piping as they're usually visible from the sides, especially at low viewing angles. You can add as much or as little of this detail as you desire.

Drill no. 80 holes in the end of the brake cylinder, two holes in the side of the reservoir, and three holes on the rear side of the control valve, **9**. Glue three lengths of .012" brass wire in the control valve, making sure that two are long enough to reach the reservoir and the third the cylinder. Glue the control valve in place and then fit the other ends of the wire to the other components and glue them in place, **10**.

Glue two brake levers in place as shown: one at the end of the cylinder rod and the other atop the center sill. I used levers from a Cal-Scale set, but you can also simply cut them from

4 Trim off the running board supports at the corners and ends. The mounting hole at the left has been plugged with a scrap piece of sprue glued in place.

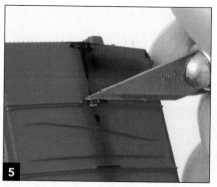

5 Trim the plug to match the existing roof texture. Start with a hobby knife and then use needle files to finish.

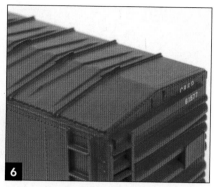

6 A couple of coats of paint help hide the roof plugs and any exposed black plastic from under the old running board.

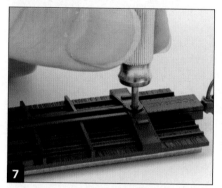

7 Tap the truck mounting holes 2-56 for the new mounting screws.

8 The Kadee coupler and spring fits in the original coupler box. The lid has been drilled out, and the hole drilled and tapped for a 2-56 screw.

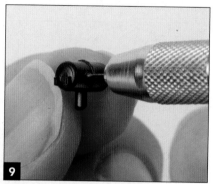

9 Drill no. 80 holes in the cylinder and other brake components to accept the new .012" wire piping.

.010" styrene (see the refrigerator car on page 91). Drill no. 80 holes in the middle and each end of both levers.

On prototype cars, brake rods run from these levers to the brake beam on each truck. On models, I glue the rod ends to the bolsters to avoid interfering with truck movement. Glue the rods in place as shown in the photos.

Secure the sheet-metal weight to the floor (double-sided foam tape works well) and glue the floor or underframe to the body.

The model's corner steps are the wrong style (angled) for the Burlington prototype, so I trimmed them off and replaced them with A-Line wire U-shaped stirrup steps, **11**. Drill no. 75 mounting holes for the new steps, making sure the holes are vertical so you don't accidentally go through the side. If the side is too thin, glue a piece of .020" to .040" styrene inside the side to provide a wider area for drilling the

mounting holes. Dip the ends of each step in a bit of cyanoacrylate adhesive (CA) or super glue and press it in place.

Add the uncoupling lever to each end. The lever goes on the left side as you're looking at the end, **11**. Drill a no. 80 hole at the bottom corner of each end and glue a wire eye bolt in place with CA. Thread the lever through the eye bolt and use CA to glue the end to the bottom edge of the coupler-box cover.

Add the brake hose. Cal-Scale's hoses include small mounting brackets. Glue the bracket next to the coupler box (on the opposite side of the lever) with plastic cement. Glue the hose in place with plastic cement as well.

Discard the car's thickly molded brake wheel and use CA to glue a new Kadee Universal brake wheel in place. Use a fine brush to paint it to match the body if needed (Kadee makes these in several styles and colors).

Decals and paint

The model's paint job is pretty good—it just needed a few decal additions. When these cars were repainted, small reflective white panels were added along the lower sides. I dug through my box of decal extras (never throw anything away from previous projects), found some extra scraps of white striping, and cut small pieces to represent these panels.

A couple of decal tips: I use an old, black plastic jar lid to hold water. It's shallow, which makes it easy for you to grab decals with tweezers, and the black color makes it easy for you to see white decals that have floated off the backing sheet. Always use distilled water for decaling—tap water can leave behind mineral stains and deposits (many modelers mistakenly think this is decal-glue residue).

Use tweezers to dip the decals in the water for several seconds and set them

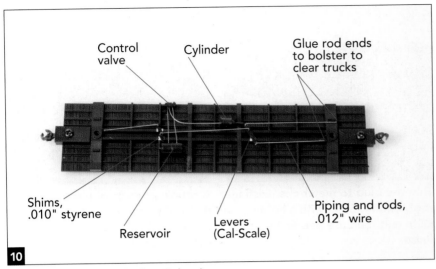

Control valve

Cylinder

Glue rod ends to bolster to clear trucks

Shims, .010" styrene

Reservoir

Levers (Cal-Scale)

Piping and rods, .012" wire

10

Mount the underbody details as shown.

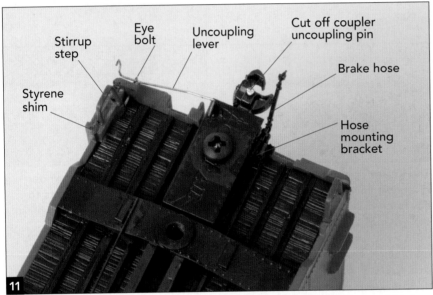

Stirrup step

Eye bolt

Uncoupling lever

Cut off coupler uncoupling pin

Brake hose

Styrene shim

Hose mounting bracket

11

Add the uncoupling levers and brake hoses. The styrene shim provides more room for drilling the step mounting holes.

Materials

Accurail
3216, Chicago, Burlington & Quincy 40-foot steel boxcar

A-Line
29000, Stirrup steps

Cal-Scale
190-276, Brake hoses
190-283, AB brake set

Detail Associates
2206, Wire eye bolts
2504, .012" brass wire
6215, Uncoupling levers

Herald King
LUBE-1, Running board decal (alternate: Microscale 87-2)

Kadee
58, Couplers
2023, Brake wheel, universal

Reboxx
33-1-1025, 33" semi-scale wheels

Sunshine Models
Chalk mark decals (alternate: Clover House 9911-01)

on a paper towel for a minute until the decal glue releases. Use a brush to dab a bit of Microscale Micro Set on the model, then place the decal, and set it into proper position. When it appears dry, add Micro Sol (a stronger solution) and leave the decal alone until it sets.

The yellow KEEP OFF ROOF NO RUNNING BOARD decal is from an old Herald King set. A reasonable substitute is Microscale data set no. 87-2.

I added several chalk mark decals to each side. You can see several of these on the prototype car—through the 1960s, agents and crew members used chalk to label cars with train numbers, track assignments, and other instructions. Sunshine Models has

offered several excellent sets of these (which I used), Microscale includes them on some decal sets, and Clover House offers a dry-transfer set for them.

Once all of the decals are dry, give the body a light coat of clear flat or semigloss finish. If I'm doing several models, I generally use my airbrush and Model Master Acryl clear flat or semigloss (thinned about 20 percent with water). For a single car, I usually just pull out a spray can: my favorites are Model Master clear semigloss (no. 1959) or Krylon clear matte finish.

Paint the underframe, including all details. For this model, I used a brush,

and mixed black and grimy black about 50/50. Paint the truck sideframes with the same black/grimy black mix. You can also add some dark brown (roof brown works well).

I replaced the original plastic wheelsets with Reboxx semi-scale (.088"-wide-tread) metal wheelsets. These look better, run better (the heavier metal wheels lower the center of gravity), and stay cleaner than plastic wheels—the metal wheels essentially polish themselves as they travel along the track.

Paint the wheel faces a shade of dark brown to black. On old solid-bearing trucks like these, the grease from the journal boxes often splattered on the wheel faces, giving them an oily, shiny look. Add the trucks to the model, and it's ready to head out in your next freight train.

Kitbashing a Monon 50-foot PS-1 boxcar

By Mont Switzer

This HO Kadee boxcar was kitbashed and repainted to represent one of Monon's 50-foot PS-1 boxcars that the railroad placed into service in 1957.

In 1957, the Monon Railroad purchased 50 Pullman-Standard PS-1 50-foot boxcars, nos. 1701–1750. At Monticello, Ind., the Monon used these high-capacity cars to compete with highway carriers for loads of finished television cabinets produced by the local RCA plant. The boxcars were the last to be delivered by a car builder in the Monon's distinctive signature paint scheme featuring THE HOOSIER LINE slogan in black letters painted on a 24"-wide light gray stripe painted across the top of the car sides.

To build this car, I started with an HO Kadee kit (no. 4105) for a 50-foot PS-1. I was looking forward to working with a model that had trucks, couplers, and details that did not require a lot of extra work, **1**. While looking over the Kadee kit, however, I found that it was not a dead ringer for the Monon prototype, **2**.

The model required backdating to match the Monon prototype. The door openings had to be narrowed from 9 feet to 8 feet, and the doors swapped for PS design doors (which feature raised panels). The modern, full-length

In November 1966, Monon boxcar no. 1744 has faded a bit but still wears its original paint scheme and number.

side sill skirts needed to be trimmed to a tabbed design. I also had to build up the underframe to match the new door and side sill configuration, and apply Monon's signature paint and lettering scheme.

I started by airbrushing the body with a light coat of flat light gray primer that would show pencil marks, knife and saw cuts, and any mistakes. It also made the gray stripe easier to apply.

Side sill modifications
The Monon's 1957 cars had tabbed side sills, while the cars represented by the kit have a continuous deep sill linking the bolster tabs. The simplest way to transfer the dimensions for the new tab side sill configuration to the solid side sill model is to draw it on the new car with a sharp no. 2 pencil, **3**. Then cut away the excess material using a fine hobby saw, hobby knife, or a scraper with a single-edge razor blade.

Use a pencil to mark the top base line on each body side so that it is even with the top of the lower door tracks and even with both ends of the side sills.

Then establish the bottom bolster tab lines by "tack" cementing Evergreen .100" L-angle styrene strip to the bottom of the center side sills. Then locate the bolster tab centers halfway between the two rivets on each bolster. Mark the bolster tab centers with a vertical line and use the dimensions in photo **3** to mark the outline of the tab.

The smaller cross member sill tabs are located at the ends of the first small cross members toward the center of the car from the bolster sill tabs. Measure

along the top base line inward from the centers of the bolster tab centers .620" and mark these point to establish the centers of the cross member sill tabs. The top of the tab is .170" and the bottom is .070". However, these small tabs are not as deep as the bolster tabs so measure down .060" from the top and draw a horizontal line across the bottom of each. Then file off the excess material.

You can also use .040" x .080" styrene for tabs, trimmed to the proper shape. I've done this with the small tabs shown in photo **4**.

Replace the .100" angle that was tacked into place with a .060" angle cemented to the bottom of the sill in the same manner. The top of the angle establishes the bottom of the center side sill. Run a sharp hobby knife along the angle several times to establish a path for removing the excess material below this line. You can then continue the knife strokes or finish the job with a fine saw.

Measure and cut the long, straight side sill, **3** and **4**. The door opening is centered over the sill.

Doors
The doorjamb details molded in-place for the 9-foot doors are not needed for the 8-foot door openings, so I removed them with a chisel-tip knife and wet-sanded these areas smooth. Add .020"-thick sheet styrene behind the vertical edges of each door opening, extending the material .100" into the opening, **5**. Bring these flush with the car sides with layered strips of .040" x .100" and .010" x .100" styrene strip overlays, bringing the filler

strips to the full .050" carbody side thickness.

Let these dry thoroughly and then fill any gaps or gouges with plastic body filler such as Squadron Green and wet-sand these areas to a perfectly smooth finish. Once the rough sanding is finished, use 400-grit and then 600-grit wet/dry sandpaper.

Trim the door tracks as in photo **5**. Slice the doorstops off with a single-edge razor blade or chisel blade. If you're careful, you can save them and move them to the left against the newly shortened door tracks. You can also cut new doorstops from .020"-thick sheet styrene using the originals as a sizing guide. Glue them at the ends of the door tracks.

Make new left doorjambs on each opening from .020" x .040" strip styrene cut to a length of 1.45", **6**. With the Kadee doors installed and in the closed position, place the jambs against the doors with the .020" sides down. Use a brush to apply liquid plastic cement to the new jambs from the sides opposite the doors, and then slide the doors back so they don't get glued to the jambs. When the cement dries, add a vertical row of Archer Fine Transfers resin rivets to the left of the jamb. These come on decal paper, and are applied like regular decals. As photo **6** shows, this row of rivets runs the full length of the jamb. The decal film will disappear as soon as the first coat of paint is applied.

The numerous body changes have all but eliminated the rivets that were molded on the car sides, and those remaining may not be in the proper locations so remove them with a chisel blade and sand the areas smooth. Apply Archer rivets to replace them. There are six rivets (3 x 2) on either side of the door opening just above the door track level, four rivets left of the door at the end of the center side sill, and two rivets on each bolster tab. You can use the former rivet locations as a guide.

Underframe
The Kadee kit has a metal floor that provides the necessary weight and correct wheelbase, but the lighter tab side sill requires a new lighter under-

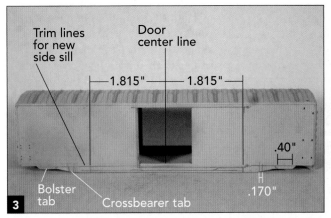

3 Draw horizontal lines marking the top and bottom of the new sill and sill tabs, as well as the locations of the bolster tabs and crossbearer tabs.

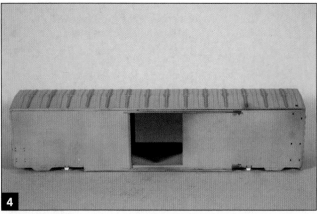

4 The side sill has been trimmed, and new styrene pieces serve as the new crossbearer tabs.

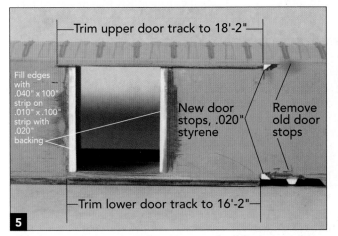

5 The door opening must be narrowed with styrene. Use putty to fill any remaining gaps and then wet-sand the areas until smooth.

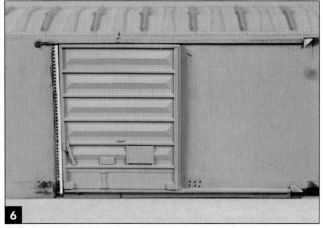

6 Add a new door jamb of .020" x .040" strip. Add Archer rivets along the new jamb and at the bottom of the sides along either side of the door.

frame that will fit behind the new tabs. Determine the B end of the metal floor (the B end of the car is the one with the handbrake). Keep the kit's truck bolsters, sill steps, couplers, coupler pockets, and brake gear. Set the brake components aside.

Now remove everything between the bolsters and start over. Begin building the replacement underframe by cutting a new center sill from Evergreen styrene .125" angle, **7**. Cut two pieces to fill the space between the two bolsters, **7**. Trim the top flanges on each to a width of .080" and glue them back to back to the metal floor with cyanoacrylate adhesive (CA). Install .080" spacers between the center sill rails and secure them with liquid plastic cement.

The eight large cross members are cut from .020" x .080" styrene, **8**. Notch one end to fit under the center sill

flange and trim them at the edge of the floor. Trim them as shown with a single-edge razor blade and glue them in place to the metal floor with CA. Touch a brush loaded with liquid plastic cement where they butt to the center sill.

Cover these cross members with caps of .010"x .040" styrene, **7**. These should extend completely across the underbody. Cut them longer than needed, glue them in place, and then trim them at the edges of the floor.

Make eight smaller cross members from .060" styrene I beams, **8**. Cut them long enough to slide under the center sill flange and reach to the edge of the floor. Trim one end of each at a 45-degree angle with a sharp blade. Glue them in place with CA as photo **7** shows.

Glue the brake gear in place, **9**. I omitted the train air line because it is

not seen. Leave as many of the air lines and brake rods attached as possible to preserve the attachment details. Trim the brake rods and air lines as necessary to achieve the desired fit. I added two air lines made from .015" brass wire which I inserted into no. 75 holes drilled into the air reservoir.

Install Kadee's bolster, coupler pocket, and sill step assemblies to the underbody. Then add a set of old truck sideframes on the model. This protects the underbody details from damage but keeps the model from rolling off the workbench.

The model includes a nice representation of the ASF A-3 Ride Control trucks favored by the Monon. I did, however, swap out the supplied RP-25 profile wheelsets for better-looking semi-scale (.088" wide wheel) versions from Kadee.

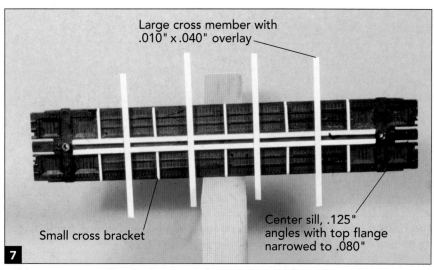

Large cross member with .010" x .040" overlay

Small cross bracket

Center sill, .125" angles with top flange narrowed to .080"

7

Add new center sills of styrene angle and then add small and large crossbearers and caps.

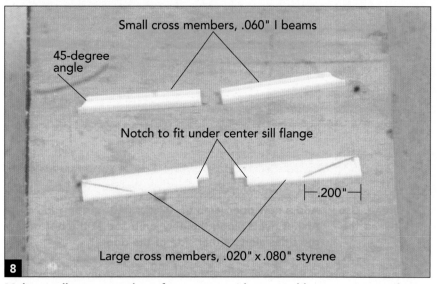

Small cross members, .060" I beams

45-degree angle

Notch to fit under center sill flange

.200"

Large cross members, .020" x .080" styrene

8

Make small cross members from styrene I beam and large cross members from styrene strip as shown.

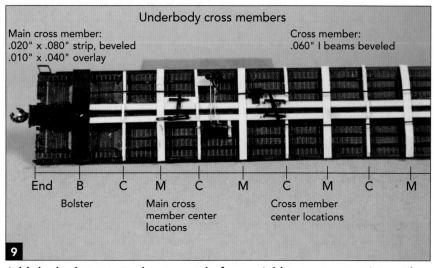

Underbody cross members

Main cross member: .020" x .080" strip, beveled .010" x .040" overlay

Cross member: .060" I beams beveled

End	B	C	M	C	M	C	M	C	M

Bolster

Main cross member center locations

Cross member center locations

9

Add the brake gear to the new underframe. Add styrene mounting pads for the cylinder, reservoir, and control valve as needed.

Paint the sideframes grimy black; if your trucks have separate brake beams clipped to them, paint them black and paint the brake shoes a rust color. Weather the area around the spring pack with Bragdon weathering powders. Paint the wheel faces, axles, and backs grimy black. Set the trucks aside until you are ready for final assembly. (You can also sandblast plastic truck frames to get a realistic appearance. See the project on the Illinois Terminal flatcar on page 85 for details.)

Painting

I used Scalecoat II paints: MOW gray for the stripe, PRR freight car red for the car sides, and black for the roof, ends, and underbody. Start by airbrushing MOW gray paint to the upper half of the car sides, doors, and side ladders. Allow this color to dry overnight and/or until the paint solvent smell is gone.

I prefer Scotch blue painter's tape for masking. The tape for masking the gray stripe should be a scale 24" wide. When masking the doors off the car, fit the tape just above the first horizontal rib and cover the remainder of the upper door. The gray bands on the car sides should line up when the doors are installed.

The removable door, ladders, and grab irons make masking the gray band, back ends, and roof considerably easier because the tape can be pressed down firmly. Airbrush another light coat of the light gray paint along the edges to seal the masking edges. Allow this gray to dry overnight, then airbrush the car sides, side ladders, and side grab irons PRR freight car red. If necessary, apply another coat where the first coat may be thin. Again, allow it to dry overnight.

Don't remove the masking tape, but instead, add to it! Wrap the newly painted sides in clean lint-free paper using small amounts of masking tape along the ends for a sharp edge, **10**. Cut the paper long enough that it folds under the side sills. When all of the white and red paint on the sides have been masked and sealed, airbrush the underbody, ends, roof, end ladders, and details with black paint. Take your time—all these areas must be sprayed from several directions to get complete coverage.

Assembly and detailing

On Kadee kits, details can be pressed into their premolded mounting holes. If they come loose, they can be secured with solvent cement or CA. The end of the body with the most holes is the B end. Make sure the floor is installed with the brake cylinder pointed toward the B end. Install a black Kadee Ajax brake wheel, which is what the Monon used on their cars. Apply touch-up paint to any details that need to match the part of the carbody where they are installed. The running board is a galvanized color that you can simulate with a flat aluminum and/or gray primer with a bit of rust added.

Decals and finishing

Apply Model Railroad Supply Monon decals in the usual manner. Apply Microscale Micro Set where you intend to place the decals. Once a decal is placed and free of trapped bubbles, apply Microscale Micro Sol decal-setting solution over the top of the decal. Once it's dried, inspect the decal for bubbles and/or glazing of the film. Lance any bubbles with a sharp model knife and repeat the application. If the decal film is glazed, apply Micro Sol again and then slice the film in the glazed area with a sharp model knife

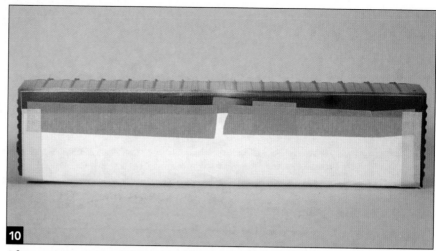

10

After painting the gray and red layers, add additional masking with both paper and tape before painting the sides and roof black.

and apply more Micro Sol. If a stronger decal-setting solution is needed, try Walthers Solvaset.

The MRS decal set (no. 301) is designed to letter several freight cars. Use two of the 40"-diameter heralds. You'll need to cut them out so that the Monon's small THE HOOSIER LINE slogan is left behind. The large MONON consists of 24" high letters and the entire word measures 13 feet in length. You will have to change the spacing of the black THE HOOSIER LINE lettering prior to applying it to the light gray band. Refer to the photos for the correct spacing.

I usually tinker with the dimensional data to show that the car was

reweighed, but these 1957 cars are so new (I model 1958–1960), I decided to apply journal repack data only. For this, I cut out small decal panels of paint that contrast with the car sides and applied one to each side. After that paint panel decal dried, I applied a journal repack decal to each side. This is a good time to add chalk marks at random with a white, yellow or light gray artist pencil to complete the car's graphics.

Once you are satisfied with your decal lettering, add trucks and any remaining details, touch-up paint, and add a top coat of Testor's Dullcote. This leaves the model with a realistic flat finish and protects the decals.

Materials

Archer Fine Transfers
AR88025, Resin rivets

Evergreen Scale Models
102, Strip styrene, .010" x .040"
105, Strip styrene, .010" x .100"
122, Strip styrene, .020" x .040"
124, Strip styrene, .020" x .080"
142, Strip styrene, .040" x .040"
143, Strip styrene, .040" x .060"
145, Strip styrene, .040" x .100"
271, I beams, .060"
291, Angle, .060"
293, Angle, .100"
294, Angle, .125" (center sill with web narrowed to .080")

Floquil Paints
11009, Primer, gray

Hi Tech Details
6026, Air hoses, 22" rubber

Kadee Quality Products
530, 33" semi-scale wheelsets, .088" wide
2040, Brake wheel, Ajax black
2225, Doors, 8' PS proprietary
4105, Boxcar, 50-foot PS-1, undecorated

Model Railroad Supply
301, Monon freight car decal lettering

Scalecoat II paint
S2020, MOW Gray
S2081, PRR Freight Car Red
S2010, Black

Testor
1160, Dullcote

Tichy Train Group
1102, Wire, .015" phosphor bronze

Undecorating a "cheese" boxcar

By Cody Grivno

1

Whichever way you slice it, Wisconsin & Southern no. 503194 is an interesting boxcar to model.

Throughout my life as a model railroader and railfan, I've crossed paths with certain pieces of equipment time and time again, and some have eventually become models for my future HO layout, **1**. As a child, it was a Burlington Northern locomotive that had a road number that matched the last four digits of our home telephone number.

Fast forward 30 years, and now Wisconsin & Southern 52-foot, double-plug-door boxcar no. 503194, painted for the cheese manufacturer Sargento, has become a frequent

subject in my camera's viewfinder, **2**. I was invited to the boxcar's unveiling ceremony (complete with a champagne christening) on November 25, 2008, in Horicon, Wis. A few weeks later, I caught up with the car in Plymouth, Wis., where it delivered its first load (Christmas trees!) during the town's Christmas festival.

Sadly, in early 2009, the car had to be stripped of its SARGENTO lettering, and the logo touting Plymouth as the World's Cheese Capitol had to be covered. Why? Because of the 1930s ruling by the Interstate Commerce

Commission that prohibited cars with advertising from interchange. But even in its patched appearance, WSOR no. 503194 proved too interesting of a modeling subject to ignore. With an Athearn HO scale boxcar in hand, I set out to re-create this one-of-a-kind car.

Removing the lettering

The first step was to remove the white SARGENTO lettering and the black OUR FAMILY'S PASSION IS CHEESE slogan. For reasons unknown to me, Microscale Micro Sol removes factory applied lettering on Athearn cars without damaging the paint. (I've tried this method on cars from other manufacturers with mixed results.) The Micro Sol works best on black and other dark colors, but it will also work on white or brightly colored graphics.

To start, I brushed Micro Sol over the slogan (but not the underline), **3**. I let the setting solution sit for several minutes until it had almost, but not completely, evaporated.

With the area still slightly damp, yet dry enough for tape to stick, I applied Scotch Magic tape over the slogan. Then I burnished the tape with a toothpick, **4**.

I slowly pulled the tape back and away from the model to remove the lettering. Not all of the lettering lifted off on the first try, so I repeated these steps until the slogan was removed, **5**.

Next, I shifted my attention to the white SARGENTO lettering, which proved to be much more stubborn. I tried removing the lettering using

On the day of its unveiling in November 2008, Wisconsin & Southern no. 503194 features lettering for Sargento Cheese.

Micro Sol and tape with limited success. Then I used a round-head toothpick to gently scrape off the lettering, **6**. This technique may remove some of the black paint underneath the lettering, but you can use a Microbrush and Model Master engine black (no. 4888) to touch up any damaged paint.

A shiny surface

With the SARGENTO lettering and slogan removed, I wiped the model with 70 percent isopropyl alcohol, followed by distilled water, to clean off any impurities that might affect paint adhesion.

I then sprayed the boxcar with Model Master gloss clear (no. 4638). This provides a glossy surface for the decals to adhere to. If you skip this

step, the decals may "silver," or fog, under and around the graphics.

Two sides, two looks

I let the gloss clear dry thoroughly (until there was no discernible paint odor). I modeled the right side of the car as it looked shortly after the lettering and slogan were removed. I cut a ⁴⁷⁄₆₄" x ⅜" piece of Microscale black trim film (TF-2) to cover the Plymouth logo. Like the prototype, the upper left corner of the patch on this side of the car is a bit wavy, **7**. The patch on the left side of the car lacks this feature.

Over time, the full-size car became the target of taggers, a look I re-created on the left side, **8**. I applied graffiti from Microscale sets 87-1139, 87-1320,

Materials

3M	Microscale	105, Micro Sol
Scotch Magic tape	MC-5004, Clean, Oil, Test & Stencil triple panels	Graffiti
	TF-2, Black trim film	
Athearn	87-1139, Urban graffiti	**Model Master acyrlic paint**
91286, Wisconsin & Southern 50-foot, double-plug-door boxcar no. 503194	87-1320, Graffiti sheet vol. 3	4637, Semi-Gloss Clear
	87-1322, Graffiti sheet vol. 2	4638, Gloss Clear
	87-1377, Burlington Northern 40- and 50-foot boxcar markings (capacity data)	4675, Rust
InterMountain		4885, Railroad Tie Brown
33" metal wheelsets		4887, Grimy Black
	87-1460, Archer Daniels Midland Trinity tank cars (for road number)	4888, Engine Black
	104, Micro Set	**Miscellaneous**
		Round-head toothpicks

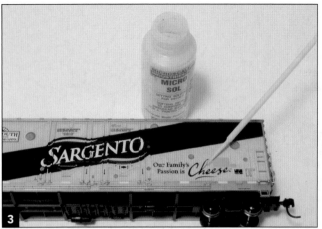

3 Apply Microscale Micro Sol setting solution to the OUR FAMILY'S PASSION IS CHEESE slogan (but not the underline). Let the setting solution sit until it has almost completely evaporated.

4 Apply Scotch Magic tape to the slogan area. Burnish it with a toothpick.

5 Peel the tape up and away from the model. If not all of the lettering comes off during the first attempt, just repeat the steps until all of the lettering has been removed.

6 The Micro Sol and tape technique didn't work so well on the SARGENTO lettering. Apply Micro Sol over the lettering and gently scrape it with a round-head toothpick. Even if you're careful, some black paint under the lettering might be damaged.

and 87-1322, **9**. I applied multiple coats of Micro Sol to help these decals conform to the boxcar's irregular surfaces.

The graffiti covered the car's road number; load limit and light weight data; and Clean, Oil, Test & Stencil (COTS) panel, just as it did on the prototype. Because this data is critical, the railroad had to re-apply it. On the prototype car, the graffiti in the affected areas was first covered with black paint. I re-created this look with black trim film, **10**. I applied Micro Sol to the trim film so it would conform to the weld seams on the model.

Then I added road numbers from Microscale set no. 87-1460 (Archer Daniels Midland Trinity tank cars),

load limit and light weight data from set no. 87-1377 (Burlington Northern 40- and 50-foot boxcar markings), and the COTS panel from set MC-5004 (COTS triple panels). As in the previous steps, apply Micro Sol to these decals so they snuggle down, **11**.

Underbody weathering

The trucks and underbody are molded in black plastic, which looks too clean, even for a recently repainted car. To give the bottom of the car an in-service look, I sprayed these parts with Model Master grimy black (no. 4887). I put plastic wheelsets in the trucks while airbrushing them so I wouldn't get paint in the sockets.

Once the grimy black had dried, I brush-painted the truck springs with Model Master rust (no. 4675). This bit of spot color makes the trucks stand out, **12**.

I replaced the supplied wheels with InterMountain 33" all-metal wheelsets. After cleaning them with 70 percent isopropyl alcohol, I painted them Model Master railroad tie brown (no. 4885) using a Microbrush, **13**.

Finishing touches

I gently wiped the boxcar with distilled water to clean off any glue from the decals and residue from the setting solution. Then I airbrushed the roof with thinned railroad tie brown

7 Apply a patch over the Plymouth logo. The wavy edge at its upper left is unique to the right side of the car.

8 In early 2009, the boxcar had its SARGENTO lettering removed. The colorful car was also tagged.

9 Assorted Microscale graffiti decals are reasonable stand-ins for the tagging on the full-size car. The logo for Plymouth is covered on this side of the car too.

10 After applying Micro Sol to the graffiti and letting the decals rest, add the black trim film patches for the road number (⁹⁄₁₆" x ⁵⁄₃₂"), capacity data (³³⁄₆₄" x ⁵⁄₃₂"), and COTS panel (²¹⁄₆₄" x ⁷⁄₃₂").

11 Brush on Micro Sol so the film conforms to the irregular surfaces and let the decals rest. Then add the road number, load limit and light weight data, and COTS panel.

12 Paint the underbody and trucks Model Master grimy black. Use an 18/0 spotter brush to apply Model Master rust to the springs.

13 Replace the stock wheels with InterMountain 33" metal wheelsets. After cleaning them, paint them with Model Master railroad tie brown, keeping the color off the treads and needlepoint axles.

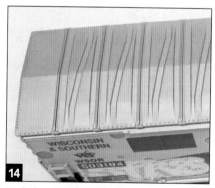

14 Lightly weather the roof using an airbrush and thinned railroad tie brown. Thin the paint 9 parts of 70 percent isopropyl alcohol to 1 part paint.

(9 parts 70 percent isopropyl alcohol to 1 part paint), **14**.

Then I sprayed the body, underframe, and trucks with Model Master semi-gloss clear (no. 4637). This seals the decal and hides their edges. In addition, the clear coat gives the car a realistic matte sheen.

With that, WSOR no. 503194 is ready for revenue service. Whether you model the car with simply the black patch over the town logo or you go all out with the graffiti, this colorful boxcar is sure to get noticed by visitors and members of your operating crew.

Modeling a C&NW ex-Rock Island boxcar

By Jeff Wilson

1

This Walthers HO model represents a former Rock Island boxcar that was purchased (and quickly repainted) by the Chicago & North Western in 1980.

When the Rock Island was abandoned in 1980, several railroads purchased former Rock Island freight cars. The Chicago & North Western bought several hundred waffle-side boxcars built for the Rock in the early 1970s. The model in this project represents one of these cars in its last days in service, **1**. The boxcar is battered, weathered, and still shows its patch-job paint scheme.

When the C&NW bought these cars, most still wore the Rock's early 1970s red scheme with large billboard lettering. The North Western wasted no time in getting these cars rolling, not bothering to completely repaint the cars. Instead, the large ROCK ISLAND lettering and reporting marks were painted over using rollers (no effort was made to match the old paint color exactly), new CNW reporting marks and numbers were stenciled in place, and the cars were placed in service.

After several years of exposure to the elements, the old lettering began wearing through the patch job. Combined with rust and other weathering, the cars took on quite a distinctive appearance as they

2

By 2002, this former Rock Island car was in wood chip service on the Dakota, Minnesota & Eastern. The old lettering shows through the quickie repaint job.

3

Cars in this service used temporary paper doors to contain the chip load. (You can see a scrap at the top of the opening.) This car has had its steel doors removed.

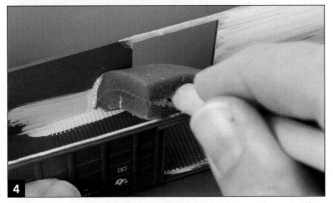

4

Paint the interior walls an off-white color such as Polly Scale SCL hopper beige. The paint job doesn't have to be perfect.

5

Paint the visible area of the floor with grimy black paint. Again, some streaks are okay to suggest a weathered appearance.

aged. By the time I photographed these cars in 2002, they had been relegated to bulk wood chip service on the Dakota, Minnesota & Eastern, **2** and **3**. Temporary paper doors were tacked across the openings (you can see the remnants in the upper corners of the door openings in these photos), and some cars even had their steel doors removed.

The model

Walthers originally released this HO car in the 1990s as an easy-to-assemble kit, and recently began offering the model in ready-to-run versions. My car is a Rock Island kit from the original run. The model is not an exact match for the prototype—the ends are different, as is the waffle pattern—but the paint scheme provided a good basis to capture the overall appearance of the prototype.

Since the doors will be open (or off), some interior painting is needed. I used a foam brush to paint the interior

walls with a beige color (Polly Scale SCL hopper car beige), **4**. I didn't mind if this was streaked, as it helped match the scuffed appearance of the real car. I gave the walls a wash of black paint (about 10 parts Polly S airbrush thinner and 1 part paint) and painted the floor grimy black, **5**.

The prototype cars have some wood chip residue visible on their floors. To model this, paint patches of the floor with acrylic matte medium and sprinkle sawdust over it, **6** and **7**. You can repeat this step multiple times to build up the effect.

The two sheet metal weights supplied with the kit are meant to be glued on the floor at each end. They would have extended into view of the doorways, so I substituted four A-Line peel-and-stick lead weights in each end (a total of 2 ounces), **8**.

Add a piece of .010" styrene across two corrugations to the left of each

door, **9**. These will hold ACI car identification panels (the plates with horizontal colored stripes) to match the prototype. Also add an AEI data tag to the lower far-right part of each side sill (visible just above the truck) as the photos show. Drill a no. 74 mounting hole and glue the Detail Associates part in place with liquid plastic cement.

To represent scraps from the temporary paper doors, I tore a piece of brown paper, and then used a small dot of super glue to secure it to the interior wall toward the top of the door opening.

I replaced the kit's horn-hook couplers with Kadee knuckle couplers. The Kadee couplers did not work well in the kit's molded coupler box, so I decided to use a no. 78 (scale) coupler in its own mounting box. To do this, remove the side walls of the car's molded coupler box with a hobby knife and then file the area smooth,

To model the remnants of a wood chip load, begin by brushing acrylic matte medium on the floor.

Sprinkle sawdust atop the still-wet matte medium and press it in place. You can repeat the process.

A-Line's peel-and-stick lead weights work well, as they can be hidden out of view in each end of the car.

A small piece of .010" styrene, cut to fit over two of the side protrusions, will hold the ACI plate decal.

10 and **11**. Place the new Kadee box in place, making sure it is centered on the mounting pad. Then mark the mounting screw location and drill an .043" pilot hole for the (supplied) 0-48 mounting screw, **12**. Screw the coupler and box in place.

The kit included basic brake gear but no pipes or rods. I added a few rods (.012" brass wire) and two levers (cut from .010" styrene)—just enough to give the impression that there's some detail under the car, **13**. I also added uncoupling levers on each end.

If you want to add more details, you can follow the example of the Burlington boxcar on pages 12–14. Paint the underbody and components with a brush or airbrush—I used grimy black.

Paint, decals, and weathering
Pick a shade of boxcar red that doesn't quite match the body color and begin brushing it over the large ROCK ISLAND lettering, making sure some of the lettering shows through, **14**. Paint out the reporting marks and car number on each side as well, and paint the styrene panel for the ACI plate. I added new consolidated stencils (the black panels with white border) that better matched the prototype. If you do this, paint the originals out with black paint.

Add the new decal reporting marks and numbers, **15**. The reporting marks are from a Microscale set for these cars (87-259), but the numbers are from a

Materials

Walthers
932-4706, Rock Island waffle-side boxcar

A-Line
13000, Peel-and-stick lead weights

Detail Associates
2206, Wire eye bolts
2504, Brass wire, .012"
6240, Uncoupling lever, modern
6246, AEI data tags

Kadee
78, Scale couplers, assembled in draft-gear box
520, 33" scale metal wheelsets, smooth-back

Microscale decals
87-1, Roman data
87-123-1, Block Gothic alphabet, white
87-259, Rock Island freight cars 1975-80
MC-4126, Consolidated stencils

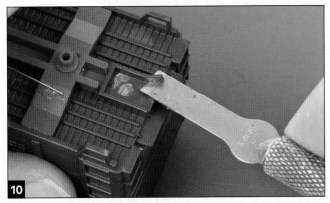

10 Use a chisel-tip hobby knife to trim away the coupler box sides and center mounting lug.

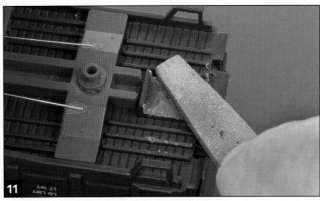

11 File the coupler mounting pad to make sure that it is level.

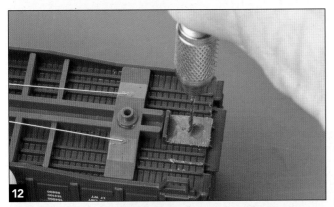

12 Place the new coupler box on the pad, making sure it's centered, mark the location of the new mounting screw, and drill a hole for the screw.

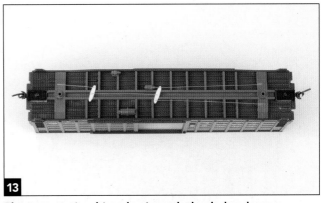

13 The car received just basic underbody hardware, including the kit's brake gear, levers from .010" styrene, and rods of .012" wire.

14 Use a wash of any shade of boxcar red to paint out the lettering, but make sure some shows through.

15 Add the new reporting mark and number decals to each side.

16 The car sides and roof received oil color washes using various shades of brown and black.

gothic alphabet/numeral set (87-123-1). The ACI plates are from data set no. 87-1 and the consolidated stencils are from set MC-4126.

I painted the truck sideframes a mix of grimy black and black. I swapped Kadee 33" metal wheelsets for the kit's plastic wheels. I then painted the wheel faces, axles, and wheel backs with roof brown.

I weathered the roof and body using rust-colored artist's oil paints (raw siena for light rust and burnt siena and burnt umber for dark rust), **16**. Dip a wide, flat brush in turpentine, touch it to a color, and streak the resulting wash down the car side. You can vary the colors and strength, and if an effect is too dark, simply go over it with another brush. You can also build the

color in layers. I gave the trucks a rusty wash as well.

On the roof, I painted patches of various rust colors and let them dry. I then gave the roof washes of rust colors and Mars black.

Let the effects dry thoroughly (a couple of days), and then give the whole model a light coat of clear flat finish.

Replicating a Soo Line 40-foot boxcar

By Keith Kohlmann

1

Soo Line boxcar no. 137608 rolls along a branch line. The N scale DeLuxe Innovations car has new body details, paint, and lettering.

Modeling a freight car built by a railroad shop usually requires many modifications to a stock model. But for this project's prototype, the Soo Line assembled the cars from components available from railroad equipment manufacturers to produce a relatively standard boxcar. The N scale AAR 40-foot boxcar from DeLuxe Innovations is a close match for Soo Line boxcars of the early 1950s, **1**. The model has 6-foot doors, an inside height of 10'-6", a diagonal-panel roof, and improved dreadnaught ends.

The Soo Line was one of the first railroads to apply billboard lettering to new freight cars built after WW II. The 4-foot-high billboard lettering first appeared in 1951 on a series of 40-foot boxcars built at the shops in North Fond du Lac, Wis., **2**. The initial batch of 400 cars featured the billboard letters centered closely around the door near the top edge of the car. Cars built in the following series had the lettering more evenly spaced across the entire side of the car, so the first group of cars stood out, making them the perfect subject for a modeling project.

2

Soo Line no. 137100 has just been completed at the railroad's car shops in North Fond du Lac, Wis., on November 9, 1951. *Trains magazine collection*

Prototype photos and several sources of lettering are available, making the project easy to complete. *Soo Line Freight Equipment and Cabooses,* by Kenneth Soros (Soo Line Historical Society, 2014), is the definitive source for how the lettering styles changed over time.

Modifying the car

Begin the project by disassembling the DeLuxe 40-foot boxcar. Gently pry the underframe from out of the body shell with a small screwdriver, and then remove the doors by poking out the door lugs from inside the shell. Pry the etched-brass running board off the roof with a hobby knife, without bending it, **3**.

If you can't find an undecorated model, remove the paint from a decorated shell by soaking it, the doors, and the running board in Scalecoat Wash Away paint remover for about four hours. The softened paint can then be gently scrubbed away with a soft

3

Disassemble an AAR boxcar from DeLuxe Innovations and strip off the paint (if it's a decorated model).

4

I glued the frame to the floor, adjusted the stirrups, filed down the bolsters, and switched out the trucks and wheelsets.

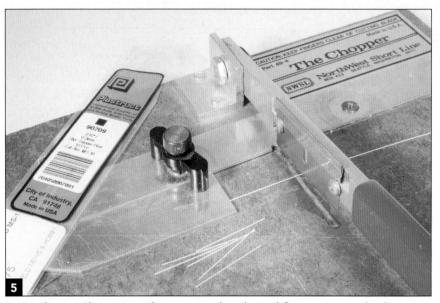

5

A Northwest Short Line Chopper is a handy tool for cutting multiple strips of .010" x .010" styrene.

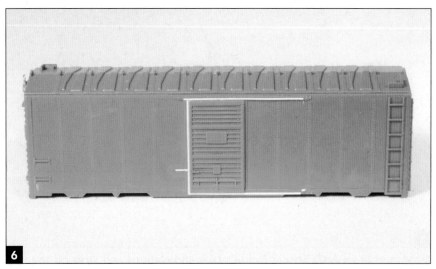

6

Use .010" x .010" styrene for the door tracks, frame, and latch.

Materials

DeLuxe Innovations
140000, AAR 40-foot boxcar

C-D-S Lettering
N-75, Soo Line 40-foot steel boxcar

Evergreen
105, Styrene, 010" square strip

Fox Valley Models
FVM-3302, Small-flange metal wheelsets

Microscale
02-0, Clear decal film
60-1, Roman style RR data

Micro-Trains
003.25.021, Brown Bettendorf trucks

toothbrush. I washed the parts with warm water and dish soap to remove the paint remover.

I trimmed and filed off the raised bit of plastic on the body bolster, filing the surface until it was level with the center sill. I replaced the trucks with Micro-Trains brown Bettendorf trucks (no. 003.25.021) and changed out the plastic wheelsets to Fox Valley Models FVM-3302 small-flange metal wheelsets. After test-fitting the trucks, I cut away areas on the underframe where the coupler box would scrape against the bottom of the car, **4**.

Using small pliers, I straightened the corner stirrups and repositioned some. I glued the frame and center sill together with styrene cement, making sure the frame was not bent when the glue dried.

Next, I trimmed flash from the plastic shell and scraped away old glue from the underside of the running board. I carefully filed flash off the ends of the running board and used a large mill file to file down the running board supports along the top of the car.

Using liquid plastic cement, I glued the doors back in place. I then added new door tracks above and below

7

This model of Soo Line 137608 represents a like-new car. It has a coat of clear gloss and minimal weathering.

the doors using 12-foot lengths of .010"-square styrene, **5**. I glued the strips directly over the raised tracks already molded into the shell. I attached a 10-foot-long strip vertically along the left edge of each door, and glued a scale 12" strip on the left side of the door horizontally for a door handle, **6**.

Painting the car

The next step was to paint the car. I airbrushed the sides, roof, and roof-walk with Floquil oxide red. After that color dried, I masked around the ends and underframe of the car and then painted them Floquil engine black. After removing the masking tape, I sprayed the entire car with a clear gloss coat. The shiny finish helps hide the decal film. To complete the painting, I sprayed a little bit of roof brown on the trucks.

I used dry transfers from C-D-S Lettering (no. N-75 Soo Line 40-foot

steel boxcar). I confess that I am terrible at getting dry transfers into the exact position, and they always end up crooked. My work-around is to burnish the dry transfers directly onto clear decal film. I rub lightly over the transfer sheet with a soft pencil to adhere the lettering to the decal paper. Then I apply a thin coat of Microscale MI-12 Liquid Decal Film over the decal sheet. This seals the dry transfers, making it possible to apply the lettering in the usual wet decal manner. I find that I get more accuracy with this technique because I can reposition the lettering on the car as much as I need to when using Microscale Micro Set decal-setting solution. Correct positioning is especially important when lining up large billboard letters across the side of a car.

In addition, I substituted dimensional data from Microscale set no. 60-1 (freight car data, railroad Roman)

for a crisper look. When the decals dried, I airbrushed the car with another thin coat of gloss finish to seal the decals and help hide their edges.

I then reassembled the car by gluing the running board in position with tiny dabs of cyanoacrylate adhesive on every roof support. I made sure the brass stirrups were in position and then reattached the body and trucks to the underframe.

I didn't apply any overall airbrushed weathering because I wanted this car to look brand new, **7**. I did brush a small amount of black weathering chalk over the sides and roof to add a little depth and shadow to the doors, ladders, and rivet details. I also added a very light dusting of white weathering powder to bring out details on the ends and in the trucks. This shiny new boxcar with billboard lettering will then mix in among the rows of weathered freight cars in the yard.

Making realistic wood grain doors

By Jeff Wilson

1

The fall grain rush means lots of traffic for rural elevators. In this HO scene, a string of boxcars with grain doors in place are ready to be loaded at a small-town grain elevator.

Through the 1960s, the most common method of carrying bulk grain was in 40-foot boxcars. Temporary doors—called grain doors—were nailed across the inside of each door opening, **1** and **2**. The elevator's loading spout was then placed over the grain doors and the car was loaded with grain. Although the process was labor intensive, boxcars were versatile cars that could be used for carrying many other goods. It wasn't until railroads were allowed to offer special rates for jumbo covered hoppers (beginning in the 1960s) that

boxcars began to give way to covered hoppers for grain shipments.

Prototype grain doors

There were two types of grain doors: wood and reinforced cardboard or paper. Wood doors were the only option into the 1950s, **3**, when single-use paper and reinforced cardboard doors began to appear. Paper doors gradually increased in popularity, and both types were used from that period through the end of boxcar grain service in the 1970s.

From the 1930s onward, wood doors were made to standard designs. Most were made from two layers of three side-by-side planks, with overall dimensions about 20" wide and 7 or 8 feet long, with a vertical piece on each side, **4**. Several grain doors would be nailed in place to the inner door posts, starting at the bottom, to the height needed for the load.

Wood doors were reusable—they would be collected at the boxcars' final destinations and shipped back to their owners. More accurately, they were shipped back to owning railroads in proportion to their use, meaning—like freight cars themselves—doors from other railroads could appear on any given railroad. To track grain doors, railroads labeled them by stenciling or stamping them with their initials, **3**, and sometimes with additional lettering, such as RETURN TO. As they aged, the wood doors would become weathered and the lettering would fade.

Modeling

Once cars were loaded, the boxcars' sliding doors were closed over the grain doors. This means that cars weren't often seen in transit with the grain doors showing, although this sometimes occurred with empty cars returning home (both sliding doors may be open, with only one side of grain doors having been removed for unloading). So if you're modeling grain doors, you're usually limited to scenes at grain elevators, inspection points, and other loading or unloading locations.

There are a few ways of modeling wood doors. You can simply glue weathered stripwood across the door openings, or you can use commercial products such as the laser-cut wood doors made by Modeler's Choice.

However, I wanted to capture more detail, specifically the stenciling found on prototype grain doors. After much experimentation, I found a relatively easy and quick method of making my own by using computer graphics and printing them out on photo paper.

In trying to figure out how to get the graphics onto the wood doors (decals, transfers, etc.), it finally occurred to me that I could just turn the doors into graphics as well. So I began by taking pieces of HO scale 4 x 10s and staining them to look like

The printed grain doors are quite realistic, showing wood grain and weathering as well as stencils that indicate ownership. The boxcar is from InterMountain.

Workers load a boxcar with a conveyor in the 1940s. The wood grain doors are stenciled RETURN TO AT&SF. *Jeff Wilson collection*

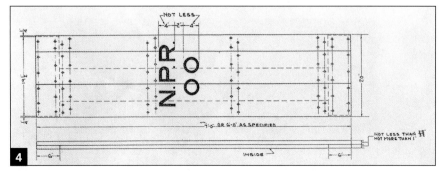

This Northern Pacific drawing shows how wood grain doors are assembled, with two layers of planks. *Northern Pacific*

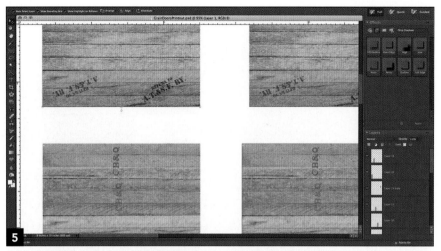

I designed my doors using Photoshop Elements. The boards are one layer of graphics, with the lettering for each door being a separate layer.

weathered wood (the size isn't critical, as the images will be later resized). I brushed the wood with a weathering mix of India ink and 70 percent iso-propyl rubbing alcohol (about two tea-spoons of ink in a 12-ounce bottle of alcohol). Some boards weathered more heavily than others—the natural varia-tions in the wood cause some pieces to be lighter and some darker.

I then placed the wood strips side by side, using a piece of tape across their backs to hold them in position, and set them on my computer's flatbed scanner. Scanning them at 600 dpi provides more than ample resolution.

You can then use any photo-editing software to combine the image of the wood strips with lettering that simu-lates the stencils applied to prototype grain doors. I used Photoshop Ele-ments, keeping the lettering as separate layers on top of the wood strips, **5**. Adjusting the opacity of the lettering layers makes it easy to have lettering that appears new or is faded.

I made several versions, for different railroads, keeping each in a strip, **6**. I adjusted the size of the doors so that each "door" (each grouping of three side-by-side boards) is a scale 20". The samples in photo **6** are printed in HO scale, so you can photocopy them for your own use (copy at 54 percent for N scale doors).

Print your doors on plain paper or matte photo paper (not glossy photo paper). I printed as many doors as I could on an 8½ x 11 sheet, cut them out, and then mounted them on .010" styrene sheet with double-sided mounting tape, **7** and **8**. This keeps them from wrinkling or bending, which makes them easier to install.

Cut a printout to the needed height and use a pencil or artist's crayon to color the top edge of the door to match the color of the printed wood. Glue the grain door inside the door opening with a bit of rubber cement or E6000 adhesive, **9** and **10**.

You can then glue the car's sliding door in place in an open (or partially open) position, **11**. By using rubber cement or double-sided tape, you allow the door to be repositioned later to appear closed.

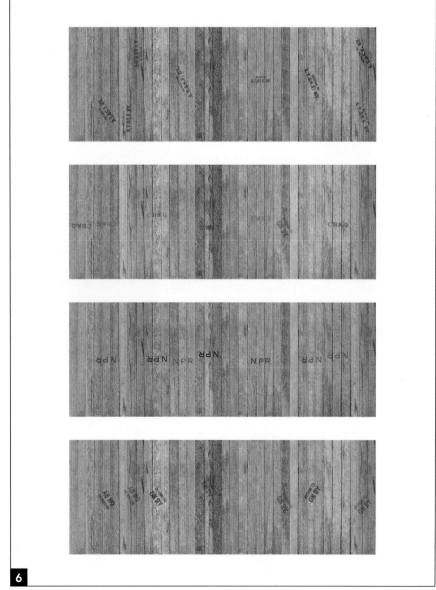

Here are samples, sized to HO scale, of grain doors with stenciling for several different railroads.

7 Print out the doors on matte photo paper or plain paper. You can print several doors on a single sheet.

8 Mount the printouts on thin styrene sheet with double-sided tape, allowing some extra material along each edge for gluing.

9 Glue each door in place in the boxcar door opening.

10 Make sure no glue is visible on the front of the grain doors.

11 Affix the car's sliding door in place in an open position with rubber cement or double-sided tape, so it can be repositioned later in a closed position.

Finishing a BN leased boxcar

By Cody Grivno

1

Not all Burlington Northern boxcars are Cascade Green. This orange Galveston Wharves boxcar has been converted into a BN lease car.

For this project, I'll show you how I converted an Athearn Ready-to-Roll car decorated for Galveston Wharves into a BN lease car using basic airbrushing and decaling techniques, **1**. If you don't have an airbrush, that's okay. You can use powdered pastels and aerosol gloss and flat coats to get similar results on your favorite boxcar from the "Incentive Per Diem" era.

For a quarter century, Cascade Green was Burlington Northern's color of choice for freight cars. But in the late 1980s and early '90s, the railroad

leased approximately 700 boxcars from ITEL, which brought new colors (and names) to BN's already impressive freight car fleet. During this time, it wasn't uncommon to see yellow (Oregon & Northwestern), dark blue (Pend Oreille Valley), dark green (Seattle & North Coast), and orange (Galveston Wharves) boxcars with BN reporting marks across the railroad's system, **2**.

A new identity

The first step in converting the Galveston Wharves boxcar into a BN lease

2 The prototype boxcar that inspired this project is shown here at the Burlington Northern yard in Crookston, Minn.

3 This is how the Athearn Ready-to-Roll car looked straight out of the box. I replaced the plastic couplers with metal knuckle couplers from Kadee.

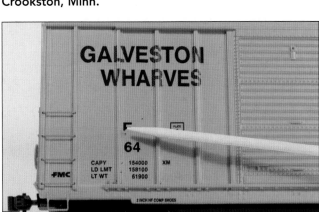

4 After soaking the reporting marks and road number with Microscale Micro Sol and letting the decal-setting solution evaporate, I used a round-head toothpick to gently scrape off the factory lettering. I also used this technique to remove the car capacity data, built date, and end reporting marks.

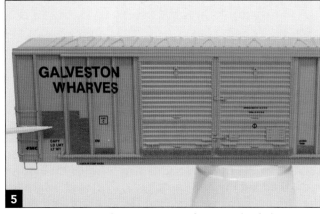

5 Using prototype photos as a guide, I masked the boxcar with blue painter's tape. I burnished the tape with a toothpick to prevent the weathering colors from wicking under the tape.

Materials

Acrylicos Vallejo
76.507, Dark Rust Model Wash

A-Line
29460, Automatic Equipment Identification tags

Athearn Trains
98404, Galveston Wharves 50-foot FMC offset double-door boxcar

Lifecolor acrylic paint
UA 758, Blackened Umber (from Burned set no. CS 29)

Microscale decals
MC-5012, Wheel dots and excess height placards
MC-5023, Miscellaneous FMC boxcar data (black)
TF-20, Light Orange Trim Film
104, Micro Set
105, Micro Sol
60-1303, Stencil lettering (for end reporting marks)
87-504, CSX freight cars (for SBD reweigh stencils)
87-1183, Chicago, Burlington & Quincy way cars (for side road numbers)

87-1335, WFCX and BNSF yellow insulated boxcars (for side reporting marks)
87-1368, Rock Island center flow covered hoppers (for end road numbers)

Model Master acrylic paints
4636, Flat Clear
4638, Gloss Clear
4675, Rust
4759, Light Sea Gray
4873, Reefer White
4885, Railroad Tie Brown
4887, Grimy Black

Moon Dog Rail Cars
WSG 001, Wheel spatter and grime decals

Polly Scale acrylic paint
414134, Undercoat Light Gray

Tamiya Color for Polycarbonate
PS-32, Corsa Gray

Weathering Solutions
1112-MST, Boxcar Roof Rust–Medium

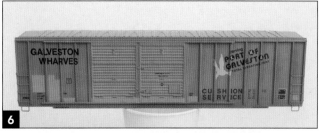

6

I weathered the car with thinned Model Master acrylic colors. Then I removed the masking tape and sprayed the car with the same company's gloss clear in preparation for decaling.

7

The full-size boxcar had been patched out two times. I applied Microscale trim film to re-create this look. Then I used assorted Microscale decal sets for the reporting marks and road numbers. As you can also see in this photo, the stirrup steps are fragile, so use care when handling the model.

8

After applying decal-setting solution to the trim film and letting it dry, I added the new capacity data from a decal set designed for FMC boxcars. The reweigh date indicates this car spent time on the Seaboard System before coming to the BN.

9

The exterior posts get scraped when the doors are opened and closed, which leads to rust forming. I captured that look by brush-painting Lifecolor blackened umber on the posts, door guides, and other areas having minor damage.

10

Although not a part of the car when first built, the Automatic Identification Tag indicates that this car operates in the modern era. The detail part is offered by A-Line as item no. 29460.

car is to remove some of the factory-applied lettering, **3**. I first soaked the side and end reporting marks and road number, the car capacity data, and built date with Microscale Micro Sol. Once the decal-setting solution evaporated, I used a round-head toothpick to gently scrape away the factory lettering, **4**. A gentle touch is all that's necessary to get the factory lettering to flake off.

Once I removed all of the lettering, I washed the shell in warm water and dish soap to remove any residue left from taking off the lettering. I rinsed the car and let it air dry on a lint-free towel. Then, using blue painter's tape, I masked the areas where the new data and trim film would be applied, **5**.

Quick and easy weathering

After the boxcar was masked, I weathered it with an airbrush. I applied thinned Model Master reefer white, railroad tie brown, and grimy black to

the entire car. I applied the brown paint heaviest along the bottom of the car to simulate dirt and dust. Grimy black works well for creating shadows along the exterior posts. I thinned all of these colors 1 part paint to 9 parts 70 percent isopropyl alcohol, which makes it easier to build up the weathering effects in light layers.

After I finished weathering the car, I removed the masks and sprayed the car with Model Master gloss clear, **6**. This provided a smooth, glossy surface for applying the decals.

Decaling in steps

Many of the Burlington Northern's leased boxcars, including the Galveston Wharves car, were on the Seaboard System before coming to the BN. In photo **2**, it appears that the car had been patched out at least twice. To re-create that look, I used Microscale light orange trim film. While I had the

decals out, I also applied the reporting marks (made by cobbling letters from a BNFE insulated boxcar set; the numbers are from a Chicago, Burlington & Quincy caboose set) and a wheel inspection dot, **7**.

With the initial decals in place, I applied decal-setting solution to the trim film. After it had dried, and I checked for and eliminated any trapped air bubbles, I applied the new capacity data from a Microscale set designed for FMC boxcars. I put together the reweigh data information from another Microscale set, this one designed for CSX freight cars, **8**.

The exterior posts in the path of the double doors are subject to damage, and those on BN no. 223437 were no exception. I simulated this look by using a 20/0 paintbrush and Lifecolor blackened umber (UA 758, part of the company's Burned color set no. 29), **9**.

11 I airbrushed the base weathering on the car but turned to decals for the rest. I used a Moon Dog Rail Cars decal set for the wheel spatters. I placed Microscale light orange trim film where the old reporting mark and road number were and compiled the reporting marks and road number from two Microscale sets.

12 Rusted galvanized metal is easy to simulate with Weathering Solutions boxcar roof rust decal set. I applied a variety of patterns to this car, using prototype photos of similar boxcars as a placement guide.

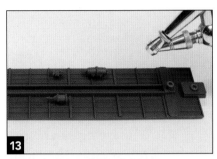

13 A quick coat of Model Master grimy black was sufficient for weathering the boxcar's underbody. Except for the air reservoir, most of the underbody detail is obscured by the car's sill.

14 Most model paints don't stick well to slippery engineering plastic. I used Tamiya Color for Polycarbonate Corsa Gray to prime the trucks before spraying them grimy black. I masked the sockets with plastic wheelsets.

15 I brush-painted the bearing caps and roller bearing adapters with Model Master paints. I applied two coats of Acrylicos Vallejo Dark Rust Model Wash to the springs, and painted the InterMountain 33" metal wheelsets railroad tie brown with Dark Rust Model Wash.

The final detail I added to each side was a small one, the Automatic Equipment Identification tag. After painting the A-Line part (one per side) Polly Scale Undercoat Light, I drilled a hole for the plastic casting using a pin vise and a no. 79 bit. Then I installed the tags with cyanoacrylate adhesive (CA), **10**.

The ends and roof
I also used the light orange trim film on the ends, where the original reporting marks were located. I masked a rectangle below the old reporting marks for the BN marks. Then I turned to Moon Dog Rail Cars decal set WSG 001 to suggest grease and oil spatters kicked up when the car is in motion, **11**.

This car also gave me an opportunity to try decals from Weathering Solutions, which I found at a local hobby shop. Weathering Solutions offers a variety of rust patches, graf-

fiti, and other specialized weathering decals. For this car, I used Boxcar Roof Rust–Medium (set no. 1112-MST), which includes a variety of random rust patterns. I followed the included direction sheet closely, and was happy with the results, **12**. This is a big time-saver since the days when I simulated rusted galvanized metal with artist's oil paints.

Underframe and trucks
The sill hides most of the underbody, so I gave it a quick coat of Model Master grimy black using an airbrush, **13**.

I also used grimy black for the trucks, but I needed to take an extra step before applying the color. The boxcar's trucks are made from slippery engineering plastic. Few model paints stick well to this type of plastic, so I primed the trucks with Tamiya Color for Polycarbonate Corsa Gray, **14**. Once that color dried, I was able to apply the grimy black.

Turning to a prototype photo as a guide, I used Model Master rust and light sea gray to highlight the roller bearing caps and bearing adapters. I highlighted the springs with two coats of Acrylicos Vallejo Dark Rust Model Wash. I painted the InterMountain 33" metal wheelsets railroad tie brown and followed it with a coat of the Dark Rust Model Wash, **15**.

Ready for service
I gently wiped the model with distilled water to remove any impurities. Then I airbrushed the body shell with Model Master flat clear. This not only hides the decal edges, but it also protects the weathering.

After the flat coat dried, I then reattached the body shell to the underframe and put the car into service. This orange car will certainly add a splash of color to my sea of BN Cascade Green.

Weathering a war-emergency hopper

By Jeff Wilson

1

Distressing and weathering boards are the key to realistically modeling a wood-sided car that's been in service for many years. This is a stock Proto 2000 HO car that's been weathered heavily.

During World War II, steel was at a premium, so railroads that built cars had to substitute other materials for steel wherever possible. The result was the war-emergency composite car: hoppers, gondolas, and boxcars that were built to then-current standards, but with wood planking substituting for steel side sheathing, **1**. Many of these cars survived into the 1960s and 1970s, albeit looking quite weathered, as the prototype photo shows, **2**.

My HO model is lettered for the Chicago, Burlington & Quincy, but you can use these weathering techniques on a car with any road name. The CB&Q built 1,000 of these cars at its Havelock, Neb., shops in early 1944. Many remained in service through the 1960s. The prototype photo shows one of these cars in 1967, highlighting wear to the boards and lettering, and it also has a sheet metal patch applied to one panel. I had a Proto 2000 ready-to-run version of this car, and I decided to try to duplicate the weathering of the real thing.

This composite-side war-emergency hopper, built in 1944, shows its age in this mid-1960s photo. The boards show lots of texture, with a significant patch at the top of one side panel. *William Raia*

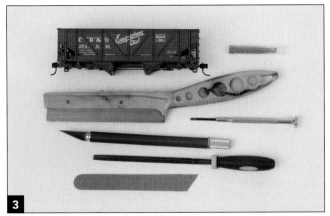

A variety of tools can be used to distress car sides, including a wire brush, razor saw, screwdriver, hobby knife, file, and emery stick.

Scraping boards with the side of a razor saw creates heavy gouges and grain lines.

Body

The Proto 2000 car has very nice detail, with separately applied grab irons, brake components, and piping. The only things I added were Detail Associates uncoupling levers and Cal-Scale brake hoses on each end. For the uncoupling lever, drill a no. 80 hole and mount an eye bolt in the lower left corner of each side. Thread the uncoupling lever through the eye bolt and glue the bottom end of the lever to the underside of the coupler box cover (see the Accurail boxcar on pages 13–14 for details). Glue the mounting pad for the brake hose next to the coupler box on the side opposite the uncoupling lever and then glue the brake hose in place.

Paint the uncoupling lever boxcar red to match the car (it doesn't have to match exactly). Paint the hose grimy black, and the glad hand (end) medium gray.

To create the weathered, worn appearance of the car, I used a combination of carving tools and paint. After several years of service, the boards appear weathered, with lots of texture, missing paint, and worn and missing lettering.

I used a variety of tools to distress the boards, including a razor saw, wire brush, emery board, screwdriver, small file, and hobby knife, **3**. The razor saw is good for creating large gouges and wood grain, **4**. I put a piece of tape over all but the end ¼" or so of the blade and then scraped it horizontally along several random boards. Do this several times and apply varying amounts of pressure each time.

The wire brush works well for creating smaller grain effects, and takes the lettering off gradually with multiple passes, **5**. For heavier gouges, I scraped boards with the tip of a hobby knife

blade or a fine screwdriver; I also cut a small emery board (a common disposable nail file) with an angled tip and roughed up several boards with it, **6**. You can mix these effects for varied looks: for example, smoothing out some of the heavy razor-saw gouges with the emery board.

Follow this distressing by painting individual boards various shades of grimy black, light gray, and dark gray, **7**. This simulates areas where the paint has worn away, exposing weathered wood underneath. I used washes on some boards, others I drybrushed or lightly streaked, and some boards I painted with full-strength paint. Again, vary this effect based on how old you want the car to appear. Brush some dark rust colors (roof brown or rail brown) along some areas of metal components, such as the side framing.

5

A wire brush makes lighter gouges and works well for removing and fading lettering.

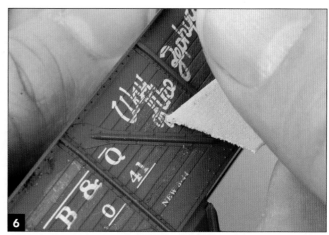

6

Cutting an emery board at an angle lets you get into corners and makes lighter gouges and marks along boards.

7

Paint individual boards with washes, drybrushing, and streaks of various shades of gray.

8

The patch is a piece of .005" styrene. Make dimples with a scriber to simulate rivet or bolt heads on the opposite side.

Materials

Walthers
920-23845, Proto 2000 war-emergency hopper, Burlington

Cal-Scale
190-276, Brake hoses

Detail Associates
2206, Wire eye bolts
6216, Uncoupling levers

Sunshine Models
Chalk mark decals (alternate: Microscale 87-228)

Woodland Scenics
B92, Mine-run coal

The car in photo **2** shows a sheet metal patch applied to the top of a side panel. I duplicated this with a piece of .005" styrene, cut to fit with simulated bolt or rivet heads applied from the rear side with a scriber, **8**. Paint this a shade of boxcar red (it doesn't have to be an exact match for the car) and glue it in place with super glue, **9**.

I added chalk marks to each side from a Sunshine decal set. These were used by agents and crews to note train numbers, track assignments for switching, and other information, and they were often found on cars through the 1960s.

Give the sides a wash of black paint, **10**. I mixed black and grimy black 1:1 and then thinned that mix with about 9 parts thinner or water. Apply it with a wide brush. The color will settle into the grooves between boards, along

gouges in the boards, and along the framework and other details. It will tie all of the distressing and other weathering together quite nicely.

When the sides are dry, apply the wash to the ends, couplers, and trucks. Paint the wheel faces dark brown (roof brown or rail brown). Once this dries, give some wheels a wash of black to simulate the grease that escapes the journal boxes and splatters on the wheels.

Coal load

It's easy to add a coal load to almost any open hopper car. Start by cutting a piece of foam to the size of the opening. I used foam core—you can use extruded or expanded foam as well. This load can easily be made removable based on how tight the fit is.

9 Paint the patch boxcar red, test-fit it, and then use super glue to secure it at the top of a side panel.

10 Give each side a wash of black and grimy black. The wash blends the rest of the weathering and highlights details.

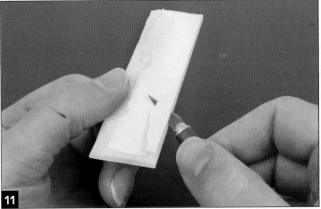

11 Cut a foam piece to fit the car and then carve it so it is raised in the middle to duplicate the center heaping of a prototype coal load.

12 Tape the load to the bottom of a shallow box and give it a heavy coat of black paint.

13 While the paint is wet, sprinkle scale coal over the load and press it in place.

14 Set the load in the car, and glue styrene spacers under each end of the load to raise it to the desired height.

Cut a piece of foam so that it slides into the top of the car. Carve the top of the foam with a knife or rasp so it is heaped in the middle, **11**. Tape the foam to the bottom of a small box (I used an old freight car kit box) and paint it with a heavy coat of black paint, **12**. While the paint is still wet, sprinkle scale coal onto the paint and pat it down, **13**. Then set it aside to dry.

You can add additional scale coal on top, seal it by using an eyedropper to soak it with rubbing alcohol, and then use another eyedropper to dribble thinned white glue (1 part glue to 3 parts water) over it. This allows a great deal of control over the shape of the load.

Let the load dry and then test-fit it in the car, **14**. You may have to do a bit of additional filing or carving of coal pieces at or near the edge of the load. Your car and load are then ready for your layout.

Decorating an ACF covered hopper

By Cody Grivno

1

I painted, decaled, and weathered this Accurail kit based on a prototype photo. Though undecorated models aren't as common as they used to be, they make it easy to model the cars you want, which comes in handy when you model an uncommon or freelanced railroad.

I model the Minnesota Northern Railroad (MNN) in HO scale, **1**. The shortline railroad, based in the northwest corner of the Gopher State, used to have a fleet of second-hand covered hoppers from Union Pacific, BNSF Ry., and their predecessor roads, **2**. It's a pretty safe bet that I'm not going to walk into a hobby shop and find MNN cars on the shelf. But with undecorated kits, hobby paints, and decals, I can add MNN cars to my fleet quickly and economically.

Though undecorated models aren't as common as they once were, they're still around, but you may have to do some searching. For this project, I used an Accurail American Car & Foundry 4,600-cubic-foot-capacity covered hopper. Athearn, Atlas, Tangent Scale Models, and Wm. K. Walthers, among others, offer undecorated models in kit and ready-to-run form.

What's in a kit?

Whenever I open a kit, I do a quick parts inventory to see if everything is included and in good shape, **3**.

Don't feel obligated to use all the parts included with the kit. I replaced the

2 The Union Pacific shield herald leaves little doubt about this car's previous owner. Minnesota Northern no. 800671 is shown at the shortline railroad's yard in Crookston, Minn.

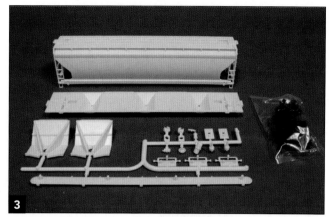

3 The Accurail HO scale covered hopper kit includes a one-piece body, separate underfame, and a sprue of separately applied parts. The plastic bag contains the trucks, wheels, couplers, and screws for securing the trucks and draft-gear box covers.

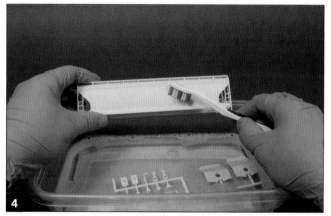

4 A paint job can be ruined if the model isn't clean. I washed the model in warm water and dish soap. After rinsing the model, I let it air dry on a paper towel.

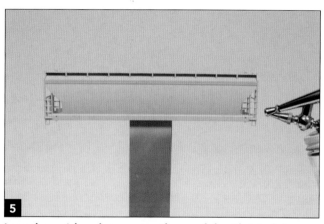

5 I used an airbrush to spray the model with Model Master camouflage gray. A paint handle makes it easy to rotate the model and ensure even paint coverage.

plastic wheelsets with 36" metal wheelsets from InterMountain and swapped out the plastic Accumate couplers for metal no. 148 whisker couplers by Kadee.

Next, I used plier- and tweezer-style sprue cutters to detach the slope sheets, hatch cover, and discharge gates from the sprue. I cleaned up rough spots, where the parts attached to the sprue, with jeweler's files and sanding sticks. I left the remaining smaller parts on the sprue so they'd be easier to paint.

I then washed all of the parts in warm water with dish soap added, **4**. This removes impurities from the manufacturing process, skin oils, and dust that may affect paint adhesion. After rinsing the model, I let it air dry on a lint-free towel. For the duration of the project, I only handled the model while wearing nitrile or powder-free latex gloves.

To the spray booth

With the model clean, I was ready to start painting. Normally, I'd recommend a primer coat to ensure that the final colors would cover evenly. But in this case, I was applying light gray to a white plastic model, so that step wasn't necessary.

I used an airbrush to spray the covered hopper Model Master camouflage gray, which is a close match for the gray Union Pacific applied to these cars. It's a good idea to use a paint handle so it is easy to rotate the model and get even coverage across the model, **5**. If you don't have a commercial paint handle, try using paint sticks or scrap wood. I've used both, and they work well, especially for underbodies and other items that aren't compatible with a paint handle.

I let the base color dry until there was no discernible paint odor. Then I sprayed the model with Model Master gloss clear, **6**. Two or three coats are typically sufficient to create a gloss coat. For best results, decals should be applied to a smooth, glossy surface. If they aren't, the decals may silver.

Applying decals

At this point, the shiny gray car doesn't look like much. But once the decals are added, the ordinary looking car will start looking the part of a hand-me-down hopper operated by a shortline railroad.

I lettered the car using sets from Microscale and Oddballs Decals, **7**. Although both brands are water-slide decals, they require different handling techniques.

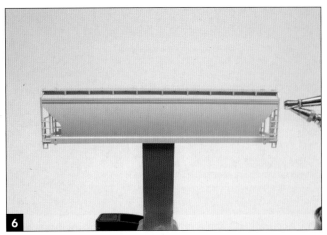

6 It's important to let paint dry thoroughly. Most modelers allow 24 hours, but I like to wait until there is no discernible paint odor. Then I applied Model Master gloss clear with an airbrush.

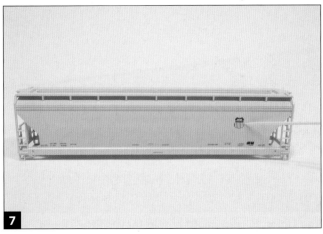

7 The plain gray car is quickly transformed with decals. I used sets from Microscale and Oddballs Decals to letter the covered hopper.

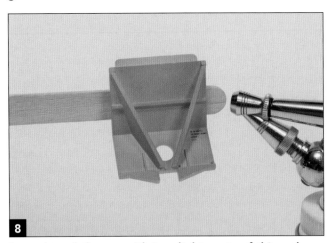

8 I weathered the car with two light coats of thinned railroad tie brown. Here, I'm weathering one of the slope sheets.

9 Take note, 3 x 5 index cards are handy masking tools. I held the card against the model and applied Southern Pacific Lettering Gray with an airbrush.

Materials

Accurail
4600, Covered hopper, undecorated

InterMountain
36" wheelsets

Lifecolor acrylic paint
UA 701, Rust Dark Shadow (in Rust and Dust diorama set CS 10)

Microscale
MC-5004, Clean, Oil, Test & Stencil triple panels (1990+)
87-850, Union Pacific covered hoppers
87-1303, Black stencil lettering

Model Master acrylic paint
4636, Flat Clear
4638, Gloss Clear
4766, Camouflage Gray
4873, Reefer White
4885, Railroad Tie Brown
4887, Grimy Black

Oddballs Decals
187-416, Union Pacific American Car & Foundry Center Flow covered hopper

Polly Scale
414179 Southern Pacific Lettering Gray

Microscale prints decal film close to the graphics. All you need to do is cut out the desired decal, soak it in distilled water for around 10 seconds, blot off the excess water on a piece of paper towel, and wait for the decal to slide freely from the paper. This usually takes around a minute. I prefer using distilled water as it's free of mineral deposits that may dry as white spots on the model.

Oddballs Decals prints its artwork directly on the decal paper. The ink is easy to damage, so I applied a coat of Microscale Liquid Decal Film to the sheet prior to use. This protects the decals from normal handling.

I cut as close as possible to the graphics on the Oddballs Decals set. A straight edge, a hobby knife with a fresh no. 11 blade, a single-edge razor

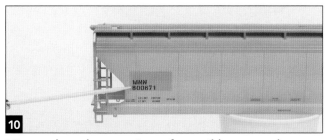

10

Microscale makes a variety of stencil letters and numbers for contemporary cars. Set number 87-1303 contained the lettering appropriate for the Minnesota Northern car.

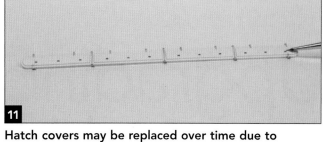

11

Hatch covers may be replaced over time due to damage. I painted the Accurail part reefer white, the hinges and batten bars camouflage gray, and the small details grimy black.

12

I airbrushed the truck sideframes grimy black, using the plastic wheelsets to mask the sockets. Then I brush-painted the roller-bearing adapters camouflage gray.

13

The steel weight included with the Accurail car may rust over time. I removed the rust with sandpaper and spray-painted the weight with rust-inhibiting primer.

blade, and a hard cutting surface (I use plate glass) are must-haves when cutting decals printed directly on decal paper. The soaking process for Oddballs Decals is the same as with Microscale.

I wet the areas where the decals will be applied with Micro Set. This setting solution helps eliminate air bubbles, which improves adhesion, and softens the decals. Once satisfied with each decal's position, I gently blotted the excess solution with a cotton swab and a paper towel.

Then I applied Micro Sol to the decals with a paintbrush. This helps decals conform to irregular surfaces. After the first application dried, I noticed a few trapped air bubbles. I gently poked them with a no. 11 blade, applied more Micro Sol, and they disappeared.

After eight hours, the recommended drying time, I gently wiped the model with distilled water to remove decal glue and residue from the setting solutions. Then I sprayed the model with a thin coat of gloss clear to seal the decals.

Weathering and patchouts
The full-sized covered hopper was fairly clean, so I weathered the model with thinned railroad tie brown (1 part paint to 9 parts 70 percent isopropyl

alcohol), **8**. I built up the effect in two light coats, and then sealed the weathering with a thin coat of gloss clear.

Next, I applied patchouts on the sides and ends of the car. Though this step looks simple, it's one I struggled finding a solution for. I thought about using Microscale trim film (solid colors printed on decal film), but I couldn't find the right shade of gray. I considered masking the patches, but I didn't want to deal with paint ridges. That's when I decided to make a floating mask using a 3 x 5 index card. I held the card against the model and applied the Southern Pacific Lettering Gray paint with an airbrush. The finished result is a patchout with sharp edges but no ridges, **9**. Since I'd be adding decals to the patches, I sprayed the car with gloss clear.

I lettered the car with a Microscale stencil letter and number set, **10**. Work from prototype photos during this step. The MNN car was neatly lettered, but that's not always the case. Patches are often hastily applied. Letters and numbers may be crooked with uneven spacing, stencils may be reversed, and there may be paint overspray around the stencils.

Older covered hoppers may have replacement hatch covers, as was

the case with Minnesota Northern no. 800671. I sprayed the one-piece Accurail casting reefer white. Then I brush-painted the batten bars and hinges camouflage gray and the smaller details grimy black, **11**.

Next, I airbrushed the entire model with flat clear to give the model a uniform finish. Then I assembled it. Though the parts are mostly press fit, I secured them with Plastruct Bondene.

Wrapping it up
I airbrushed the truck sideframes grimy black, using the plastic wheelsets to mask the sockets, **12**. Then I brush-painted the roller-bearing adapters camouflage gray. I used InterMountain 36" wheelsets on the covered hopper. I cleaned the metal wheelsets with 70 percent isopropyl alcohol before painting them with Lifecolor rust dark shadow.

The final step is optional. The steel weight included with the car is often rusty, **13**. For neatness, I usually sand off the rust and spray the weight with gray or oxide red rust-inhibiting primer.

Then I set the weight in place, gently pressed the carbody onto the underframe, and attached the trucks and draft-gear box covers. The covered hopper is now ready for service on the MNN.

Upgrading a basic covered hopper

By Cody Grivno

1 Northwestern Oklahoma covered hopper no. 822263 is part of a manifest freight on *Model Railroader*'s Wisconsin & Southern project layout.

Okay, I'll admit it. I'm a fan of covered hoppers. A sizeable number of cars in my fleet are decorated for Burlington Northern; Atchison, Topeka & Santa Fe; and BNSF Ry. This makes sense, as BNSF Ry. interchanges with the Minnesota Northern (the railroad I model) in Crookston, Minn.

To balance out my HO fleet, I need cars from other railroads and leasing companies, **1**. Though I photographed Northwestern Oklahoma Thrall 4,750-cubic-foot-capacity covered hopper no. 822263 in Pewaukee, Wis., it would certainly look right at home in a cut of cars in northwest Minnesota, **2**.

This project is more than simply patching out an Atlas Trainman Thrall 4,750-cubic-foot-capacity covered hopper, **3**. I upgraded the running boards, crossover platforms, and roping loops; replaced a stirrup step; and tried some new weathering decals.

Rooftop upgrades
First, I removed the injection-molded plastic running board assembly on the model using a screwdriver. Careful as I tried to be, a few mounting pins

2 The full-size Northwestern Oklahoma no. 822263 covered hopper is seen here in Pewaukee, Wis.

3 The HO scale Atlas Trainman model started life decorated for the Milwaukee Road.

4 I removed the plastic running boards using a screwdriver. Some mounting pins snapped off during the process, which was okay. I filled the remaining holes with .035" styrene rod. I secured the pins and rod with glue and sanded the bracket tops smooth.

5 After setting the roof back on the carbody, I touched up the running board brackets with a Microbrush and Polly Scale Amtrak Red. This proved an unnecessary step as I later removed the paint to secure the metal replacement running boards.

snapped off, but that worked to my advantage. I left those pins in their holes, and filled the remaining holes with .035" styrene rod, **4**. It's best to plug the holes with the roof separated from the model. To separate the roof from the carbody, remove the two screws in the center sill just inboard of the trucks.

I secured the pins and rod with styrene cement and let them dry. Then I trimmed the styrene flush with the brackets and sanded the mounting pins and styrene rod until the tops of the brackets were smooth.

At this point, I hadn't determined how I'd secure the stainless steel running boards. I used a Microbrush to touch up the running board brackets with Polly Scale Amtrak Red, **5**.

Carbody improvements
The primary part in Plano Model Products set no. 10790 is the stainless steel running board, but the upgrade kit also includes new crossover platforms and two options for roping loops.

I used sprue cutters, jeweler's files, and sanding sticks to remove the molded plastic crossover platforms. Do this carefully, as it's easy to remove too much plastic. With the supplied jig, a pin vise, and a no. 78 bit, I made holes for the metal crossover platforms, **6**. After I'd finished drilling the holes, I touched up the bare plastic with Amtrak Red.

To make the Trainman model more closely match Northwestern Oklahoma no. 822263, I removed the Milwaukee Road reporting marks, road number, roping loops (yes, they're printed), car capacity data, Thrall builder's stencil, and Clean, Oil, Test & Stencil (COTS) panel using Microscale Micro Sol and a toothpick, **7**.

Unfortunately, this process caused some of the black printing to rub off on the red and white paint. I corrected this by gently wet sanding the affected areas with 600-grit and 1,500-grit sandpaper. I also used the wet-sanding technique to remove the end reporting marks.

With the unwanted data removed, I switched gears and added the new

roping loops. The kit includes two styles of loops. The one I chose isn't an exact match for the prototype, but the loops are closer than what was printed on the model.

Before installing the loops, I gently sanded both sides of the metal with 1,500-grit sandpaper. This gave the metal some tooth, which helped the glue and paint stick better, **8**. After I'd installed roping loops, I brush-painted the parts with Amtrak Red and Model Master engine black.

Grime time
With holes plugged (and in a few cases, drilled), new parts added, and touch-up paint applied, I gently wiped the model with 70 percent isopropyl alcohol. This removes skin oils and other impurities that might affect paint adhesion. Then I sprayed the model with two light coats of Model Master gloss clear. This provided a smooth, glossy surface for the decals I needed to apply prior to weathering. Then I added the new Thrall builder's stencil and COTS panel, **9**.

6 I centered the jig for the crossover platform on the draft-gear box and used a pin vise with a no. 78 bit to make holes for the new part. I repeated this process on the B end of the car.

7 To avoid having to repaint the car, I used Microscale Micro Sol to remove unwanted graphics. I wet-sanded areas where the black printing left residue on the white and red paint with 600-grit and 1,500-grit sandpaper.

8 The roping holes were originally printed on the model. I used jack pad faces from a Plano kit to upgrade these areas.

9 Microscale decal sets MC-5004 and 87-1276 provided the new COTS panel and Thrall builder's stencil, respectively.

After the decals were in place, I used a cotton swab dipped in distilled water to remove decal glue and residue from the decal-setting solution. Then I sprayed the panels containing the decals with a thin coat of gloss clear to seal the decals and prevent the weathering colors from forming halos around the clear decal film.

Next, using blue painter's tape, I masked the area where the new reporting marks would be added. I then sprayed the entire model with thinned railroad tie brown and grimy black (9 parts 70 percent isopropyl alcohol to 1 part paint). I followed that with thinned engine black (same ratio) along the exterior posts. I built up the weathering in several light layers, as it's much easier to add more weathering than it is to remove some.

With the weathering applied and the masking tape still on the car, I dipped a cotton swab in Windex to do some reverse weathering. Using prototype photos as a guide, I carefully wiped some of the paint off the faces of the exterior posts, **10**. Then, keeping the swab parallel with the posts, I gently wiped paint off the body panels to re-create the look of uneven grime on these areas.

I finished this phase of the project by spraying the model with gloss clear. This not only protects the weathering, but it readies the model for the next round of decaling.

Post-weathering work

I let the gloss clear dry thoroughly (exhibiting no discernible paint odor) before proceeding. While examining

prototype photos, I noticed three of the four hatch covers had been replaced. I captured that look by brush-painting the same number of hatch covers with Polly Scale new gravel gray. To further enhance the roof, I painted the batten bars and hinges grimy black, **11**.

I lettered the car with decals from a set designed for center-beam bulkhead flatcars. The lettering is a bit smaller, but I was willing to compromise on that front because the font closely followed that the one on the prototype, **12**.

Though I had applied a general weathering coat to the slope sheets, I also wanted to add the vertical streaks of grime kicked up from the spinning car wheels. Instead of doing this with an airbrush, I used Moon Dog Rail Cars wheel spray and flange sling decals, **13**. This decal set contains

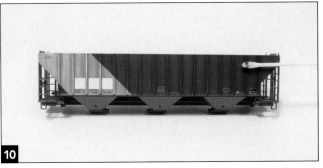

10 A cotton swab dipped in Windex is handy when doing some reverse weathering. Here, I am wiping paint off the faces of the exterior posts. I also used this technique to remove some of the weathering from the body panels (with the masking tape on, of course).

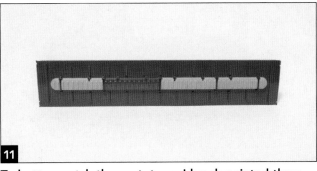

11 To better match the prototype, I brush-painted three of the four hatch covers with Polly Scale new gravel gray. I made the batten bars and hinges stand out by painting them grimy black.

12 A decal set for center-beam bulkhead flatcars contains NOKL reporting marks and road numbers in a font that is similar (but smaller) than the one used on the full-sized covered hopper.

13 Decals aren't just for lettering. I added the vertical streaks of grime kicked up from spinning car wheels using decals from Moon Dog Rail Cars.

streaks in various shades and patterns, appropriate for use on car ends on hopper bays. I applied Microscale liquid decal film to the set prior to application to protect the printing.

Unfortunately, the car suffered a bit of damage during the decaling process when one of the stirrup steps snapped off, **14**. I replaced it using a stirrup from A-Line set no. 29000, a no. 73 bit, and a pin vise. I brush-painted the brass part with Model Master Rot RLM 23.

With the decaling completed, I once again cleaned the model with distilled water. Then I sprayed the model with Model Master flat clear to seal the decals and hide their edges, as well as give the model a uniform dull finish.

Finishing touches
With the car weathered and decaled, it was time to address the running board assembly. As done before, I

gently sanded the stainless steel to promote glue and paint adhesion. I also masked the gluing faces on the bottom. Then I applied light coats of caboose red, railroad tie brown, and grimy black. I sealed the weathering with flat clear and removed the masking tape.

I sanded the paint off the running board supports so the gluing faces would be clean. Then I used a toothpick to apply E6000 glue. This glue works well for securing metal parts to plastic models, but apply it sparingly. The running boards are perforated, so excess glue will ooze out of the holes.

I wasn't happy with the airbrushed weathering on the running board assembly, so I randomly drybrushed panels with Lifecolor UA 701 rust dark shadow to capture the look of rusty, galvanized steel. In addition, I brush-painted one panel camouflage gray to suggest it had been replaced, **15**. I also used this color to paint the corner grab

irons, which I secured with cyanoacrylate adhesive (CA).

To give the crossover platforms the look of newer galvanized steel, I only weathered them with flat clear. Then I secured the parts with CA.

The trucks are molded in a shiny black plastic, which would look out of place on a weathered model. I replaced the metal wheelsets with plastic ones to mask the sockets and sprayed the trucks grimy black. Then I brush-painted the bearing caps railroad tie brown.

I cleaned the blackened metal wheelsets with 70 percent isopropyl alcohol to remove any residue from the manufacturing process. Then I painted them blackened umber using a Microbrush. I didn't paint the face of the tread to indicate that the car had recently passed through retarders in a hump yard, **16**.

Finally, I weathered the couplers using a three-step process. First, I

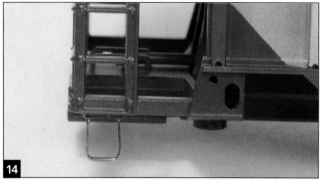

14

While decaling the car, one of the stirrup steps snapped off. I replaced it using a formed brass step from A-Line kit no. 29000.

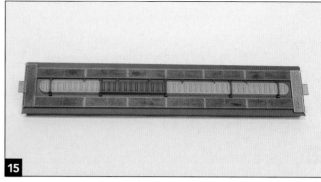

15

I secured the running board assembly with E6000 glue, making sure the gluing faces were clean. After installation, I weathered the running boards to suggest one of the panels had been replaced.

16

A quick coat of grimy black made the shiny plastic trucks look more realistic. I brush-painted the bearing caps railroad tie brown and the blackened-metal wheelsets Lifecolor blackened umber.

17

Couplers should be weathered as well. Railroad tie brown, grimy black, and a silver paint marker were all I needed to give the couplers a realistic, weathered appearance.

airbrushed the couplers with railroad tie brown. I held the airbrush away from the model so the paint was almost dry when it hit the coupler. This keeps the spring from gumming up and gives

the couplers a realistic, gritty texture. Then I brush-painted the trip pin grimy black, and touched a silver paint marker to the tip of the pin to simulate a glad hand, **17**.

With that, NOKL no. 822263 was ready to join my covered hopper fleet, and the weathered red-and-white car stands out in the sea of Cascade Green and Oxide Red.

Materials

Atlas Model Railroad
20 000 895, Milwaukee Road Thrall 4,750-cubic-foot-capacity covered hopper

Eclectic Products
E6000, Craft adhesive

Evergreen
220, styrene, .035" rod

Lifecolor paint
UA 701, Rust Dark Shadow (in set CS 10, Dust and Rust)

UA 758, Blackened Umber (in set CS 29, Burned)

Microscale decals
MC-5004, COTS triple panels (1990+)
104 Micro Set
105 Micro Sol
112 Liquid Decal Film
87-1276 Burlington Northern covered hoppers
87-1385 NOKL Leasing center-beam bulkhead flatcars

Model Master (acrylics unless noted)
2073, Rot RLM 23 (enamel)
4636, Flat Clear
4638, Gloss Clear
4766, Camouflage Gray
4880, Caboose Red
4885, Railroad Tie Brown
4887, Grimy Black
4888, Engine Black

Moon Dog Rail Cars
WSG 001, Wheel splatter

Modeling an ex-CRR aggregate hopper

By Cody Grivno

This ex-Clinchfield quad hopper is serving out its remaining years hauling aggregates for the Strata Corp.

I n the mid-1990s, ex-Clinchfield (CRR) quad hoppers made their way to Minnesota to transport aggregates for Strata Corp. Years of hauling coal and ore took its toll on the steel cars, and repairs had to be made. The interiors were relined, and rusted body panels were reinforced. This patch-work-quilt appearance makes for an interesting modeling project, **1**.

The Bethlehem Steel-built cars began their career transporting coal for the CRR. The cars continued to haul black diamonds for successor CSX before being sold to Wisconsin Central. On the WC, the cars hauled taconite and coal, **2**.

A well-traveled workhorse

For this project, I used a Tangent Scale Models' HO Wisconsin Central (ex-Clinchfield) Bethlehem Steel quad hopper, **3**. I began by wet-sanding the factory lettering off, except for the CLINCHFIELD lettering, the Automatic Car Identification labels, and the data below the reporting marks on the slope sheets, **4**. I lightly wet-sanded the CLINCHFIELD lettering to give it a worn, oxidized look.

2

BGSX no 122558 sits in the Minnesota Northern yard in Crookston, Minn. The next day, the car will be loaded with aggregates. *William Phalen, Cody Grivno collection*

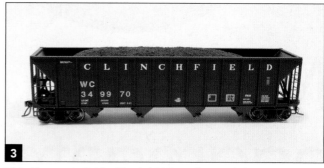

3

This Tangent Scale Model HO scale model was the starting point for my project. It is lettered for Wisconsin Central, which acquired the ex-CRR hopper.

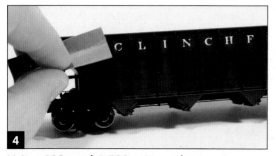

4

Using 600- and 1,500-grit sandpaper, I wet-sanded the car to remove all of the factory lettering except for the CLINCHFIELD lettering, ACI labels, and data on the slope sheets. I used the same technique to weather the CLINCHFIELD lettering.

5

This close-up is of a prototype reinforced body panel. *William Phalen, Cody Grivno collection*

6

I thoroughly washed the model to remove residue from the wet-sanding process. Then I used .010" styrene cut to fit to simulate the repaired body panels. I used medium viscosity CA to attach the styrene to the plastic.

Then I washed the car in warm water with a few drops of liquid dish soap added. This removed the residue from the wet-sanding process. While the car was air drying, I cut strips of .010" styrene to match the width of the body panels. Then I cut the styrene to the appropriate height for each panel, using prototype photos as a guide, **5**. I attached the styrene strips to the car with a thin layer of medium viscosity cyanoacrylate adhesive (CA), **6**. Make sure the styrene is aligned properly, as you only get one chance to apply it. If you use liquid plastic cement to attach the styrene to the car, apply it sparingly, as it may melt the thin styrene.

In hindsight, I should have used .005" styrene or brass for the repaired body panels. Once the car was painted and weathered, the .010" styrene looked a bit thick. Lesson learned for next time.

Interior upgrades

A friend was able to get interior shots of the full-size BGSX quad hoppers, which isn't always easy in tabletop flat

northwestern Minnesota. What the pictures revealed was quite interesting. The slope sheets and sill were lined with new steel. The fresh, grimy black metal contrasted with an otherwise rusty interior.

Since I'd be working on the interior, I removed the six interior braces using a no. 17 blade, **7**. Though the braces are glued in place, a bit of gentle persuasion with the chisel blade proved enough to break the joints.

With the braces removed, I turned my attention to the eight ejector-pin marks. I didn't want these blemishes, a result of the manufacturing process, to show when the car runs empty. I used a Microbrush to fill the marks with medium viscosity CA (I prefer CA over putty as body filler because it dries quicker and doesn't shrink). Once the CA had cured, I sanded the areas until they were smooth.

To the spray booth

With the body work complete, I washed the car one more time in warm water and liquid dish soap. This step

removes dust, skin oils, and other impurities that might affect paint adhesion.

Again using prototype photos, I masked the areas that would be weathered. Then I used an airbrush to spray the sides Model Master engine black. This not only covers the white styrene body panels, but it covers any areas where paint was removed during the wet-sanding process.

I let the paint dry thoroughly (no discernible paint odor) before masking the areas sprayed with engine black, as well as the areas where the end reporting marks would be applied, in preparation for weathering, **8**. I prefer to use blue low-tack painter's tape as it's less likely to peel up the fresh paint and leave a sticky residue.

I weathered the car with thinned (1 part paint, 9 parts 70 percent isopropyl alcohol) Model Master grimy black, railroad tie brown, and oxide red. I built up the weathering effect in light layers. It's easier to add more weathering than trying to remove too much.

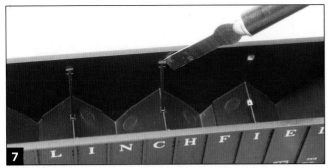

7 To make it easier to reach the ejector-pin marks on the slope sheets, I removed the six interior braces. A gentle rocking motion with a no. 17 blade was all it took to break the glue joint.

8 Once the engine black paint had dried, I masked those areas with blue painter's tape. Though no longer used, shop forces masked around the Automatic Car Identification panel on the right side of the car.

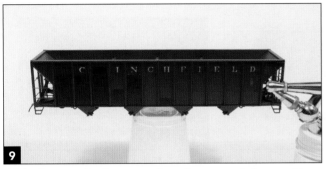

9 With the weathering complete, I removed the masking tape and sprayed the hopper with Model Master gloss clear. This photo shows the body panels I painted with Lifecolor burned black.

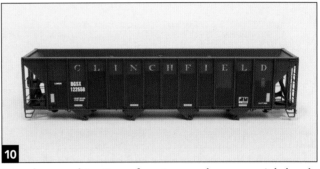

10 It took a combination of custom and commercial decals to letter BGSX 122558 as it appears today. The load limit and light weight data is correct for this road number.

When studying prototype photos, I noticed some body panels had been painted once before. To capture that look, I used a Microbrush to apply Lifecolor burned black, **9**. Then I removed the masking tape and sprayed the hopper with Model Master gloss clear to provide a smooth, glossy surface for the decals.

Adding decals

I designed the artwork for my Strata Corp. decals based on prototype photos I took during a trip to northwest Minnesota approximately a decade ago. I knew I'd need to supply the modern Clean, Oil, Test & Stencil panels, which are readily available from Microscale, among other sources. When my friend sent up-to-date prototype images, I noticed the car had the Federal Railroad Administration-mandated reflective stripes and new lettering for the car's load limit and light weight.

The yellow reflective stripes were easy to locate. I used stripes found in Microscale Decals set 87-1337 (CSX 50-foot boxcars), but they're also available in a variety of other modern decal sets offered by Microscale and other manufacturers.

The closest lettering I could find for the load limit and light weight data was in set 87-1292 (Minnesota, Dakota & Western/International Bridge & Terminal modern boxcars). Yes, I actually cut and rearranged the numbers to match the prototype car, **10**.

Lining the car. . .with paint

While I was working on the car's exterior, I continued to think about how best to re-create the look of new metal in the hopper's interior, **11**. Then it dawned on me. I didn't need thin styrene or brass. I could use paint. First, I sprayed the car's interior with Model Master grimy black, a close approximation to the color of the new metal, **12**. Once the paint had dried, I used blue painter's tape to cover the grimy black in preparation for weathering, **13**.

I carefully masked the car sides and sprayed the interior and braces with

11 This interior view of BGSX 122558 shows the repairs that were made to the quad hopper. *William Phalen, Cody Grivno collection*

Model Master leather. I followed that up with thinned railroad tie brown (mixed to the same ratio I used earlier), which I dusted along the upper sides and ends of the car and the tops of the braces.

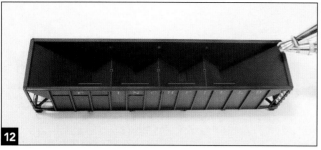

12

I airbrushed the car's interior with Model Master grimy black. This color closely matches the new metal used to line the interior of the full-size car.

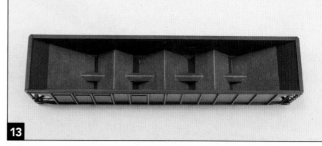

13

After the grimy black had dried, I masked the interior in preparation for weathering. I burnished the tape with a toothpick to prevent the weathering colors from wicking under the tape.

14

I weathered the car's interior and braces with Model Master leather and thinned railroad tie brown. I then removed the masking tape and used an airbrush to apply Model Master flat clear. Once the finish had dried, I reinstalled the interior braces.

15

The reinforced body panels on the prototype car have nut-bolt-washer assemblies near the top. I re-created that look using Detail Associates 2203 nut-bolt-washer castings.

After letting the paint dry for 24 hours, I sprayed the quad hopper's interior and braces with Model Master flat clear. Then I reinstalled the braces with CA, **14**.

Finishing touches

On the prototype, the raised body panels feature two nut-bolt-washer castings near the top. I added that detail to the model with Detail Associates 2203 nut-bolt-washer castings, **15**. The head of each nut and another washer are visible from the interior. Adding the interior nut-bolt-washer castings may be more effort than it's worth, especially if the car is run with removable loads.

I airbrushed the trucks grimy black, masking the sockets to keep the wheels free rolling. Then I brush-painted the roller bearing adapters Model Master light sea gray and drybrushed the springs with the same firm's leather. I also brush-painted Model Master engine black on the sideframes to suggest the old reporting marks were painted out. I used a white colored pencil to write in the BGSX road number. I used a Microbrush to paint the wheels railroad tie brown.

Finally, I sprayed the car's exterior with Model Master flat clear. Once that had dried, I installed Kadee no. 148 whisker couplers in the draft-gear boxes and reinstalled the trucks. With that, BGSX 122558 was ready for its first trip to the quarry.

Materials

Detail Associates
2203, Nut-bolt-washer castings

DM Custom Decals
Bradshaw Gravel and Sand (BGSX) custom decals

Microscale decals
MC-5004, Clean, Oil, Test & Stencil triple panels (1990+)
104, Micro Set
105, Micro Sol
87-1292, Minnesota, Dakota & Western modern boxcars (capacity data)
87-1337, CSX 50-foot outside braced boxcars (reflective stripes)

Lifecolor acrylic paint
UA736, Burned Black (in set CS27 Black Rubber Shades & Co.)

Model Master acrylic paint
4636, Flat Clear
4638, Gloss Clear
4674, Leather
4759, Light Sea Gray
4882, Oxide Red
4885, Railroad Tie Brown
4887, Grimy Black
4888, Engine Black

Tangent Scale Models
10858-01, Wisconsin Central (ex-Clinchfield) Bethlehem quad hopper

Building a PM auto frame gondola

By Keith Kohlmann

1

The Shapeways 3D printing process makes it possible for modelers to work with complicated, delicate shapes such as these auto frames, shown loaded in a modified Micro-Trains N scale gondola.

In the mid-20th century, the Pere Marquette Railway operated a specialized fleet of freight cars specifically designed to serve the automotive industry. These cars moved auto parts to assembly plants in Michigan and distributed finished automobiles and parts across North America. The PM was absorbed into the Chesapeake & Ohio Railway in 1947, and much of the equipment was re-lettered for the C&O.

The Pere Marquette's auto frame gondolas were a group of very distinct specialized freight cars, **1**. They could be spotted operating on the C&O

Lake Michigan carferry route between the A. O. Smith factory in Milwaukee and automotive assembly plants in Michigan. (In 1950, A.O. Smith manufactured almost 40 percent of all car and truck chassis frames made in the United States.) PM gondolas were used in auto frame service into the mid-1960, when the traffic was moved to flat cars.

Pere Marquette 18692

In 1941, Bethlehem Steel built 200 gondolas in the 18650–18849 series for the Pere Marquette, **2**. These 70-ton,

2

In 1941, Bethlehem Steel built 200 gondolas for Pere Marquette. These 70-ton, 50'-6" riveted cars featured 14 side posts, Dreadnaught drop ends, wood floors, and an Equipco pump-handle hand brake mounted on the corner post of the B end.

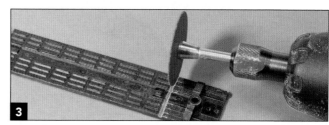

3

I cut the ends off the metal underframe insert with a cut-off wheel. You could also use a hacksaw.

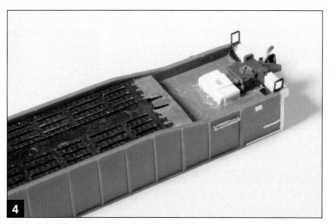

4

Then I built a new body bolster from styrene and installed couplers directly to the bottom of the car.

5

Check the coupler height with a Micro-Trains coupler gauge.

50'-6" riveted cars featured 14 side posts, Dreadnaught drop ends, wood floors, and an Equipco pump-handle hand brake mounted on the corner post of the B end. During the late 1940s and 1950s, several of these cars were fitted with steel end frames and tie-down hardware to support stacked auto and truck frames. (*Pere Marquette Revenue Freight Cars,* Hundman Publishing, 2001, is an excellent source for PM cars.)

Modifying the body

I began this project with a Micro-Trains N scale 50-foot steel-side, 15-panel, fixed-end gondola. I separated the body from the underframe and removed the plastic frame, trucks, and stirrup strips.

Use a Dremel tool or small hacksaw to cut off a scale 9'-6" from both ends of the metal underframe, **3**. File the ends smooth, and glue the underframe into place under the car. Cut off the ends of the plastic frame so it is the same length as the metal underframe, and glue it to the car.

I built new bolsters from two layers of Evergreen HO scale strip styrene. The bottom layer is made of two scale 4-foot pieces of 4 x 6 and 6 x 12, glued side by side. On top of this layer, glue a 2-foot pad, cut from a 4 x 12 strip of styrene. I glued this assembly to the underside of the car where the previous bolster was located, using a no. 47 drill bit to make a hole for each truck-mounting pin, **4**.

Next, I took the trucks from an Atlas 70-ton Hart ballast car and cut off the couplers. I drilled out the bolster hole so it could be used with Micro-Trains truck mounting pins. I did this in two steps for a more precise hole: For the first pass, I used a ⅛" drill bit to open up the hole and then followed with a ⁵⁄₆₄" bit for the finish cut. I inserted Fox Valley Models FVM-3302 small-flange wheelsets in the truck frames.

Install Micro-Trains no. 1025 couplers at each end, making sure the coupler pockets stick out a scale 6" from each end. Check the height of the couplers with a Micro-Trains coupler gauge, **5**.

Next, I used a large flat mill file to file down the upper edge around the top of the gondola. I then cut off the side ladders and grab irons with a sharp no. 11 blade.

I cut out the ends of the car with a razor saw and then filed the ends flat and the openings square, **6**. I test-fit Micro-Trains no. 1099 gondola drop ends, trimmed the bottoms, and glued them in place into each end of the car, making sure the side with three ribs faced inward. To create the end sills, I glued two pieces of .030" x .080" styrene on either side of the coupler.

Detailing

At each corner, I glued strips of .010" x .010" styrene to extend the upper rail along the top edges of the sides. I glued a strip of .030" x .060" styrene vertically at each corner.

I created new grab irons by gluing scale 30" strips of .010" x .010" styrene at the corner sides and ends. While the plastic was still soft from contact with the plastic cement, I pressed the back-side of a no. 11 knife blade into the

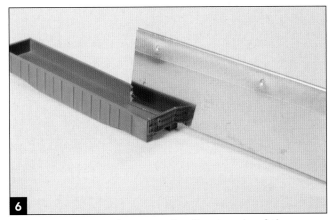

6 Using a razor saw, I cut out the fixed ends of the car.

7 Next, I glued a strip of styrene along the top of the car at the corner. I made the flanged brackets from porch railing.

8 I built up the ends of the car with styrene and glued a handbrake and a step to the corner of the B end.

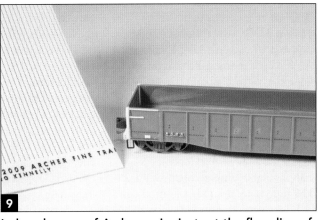

9 I placed a row of Archer resin rivets at the floor line of the car.

grabs to create a flat spot 1 scale inch in from the ends. This makes the ends of the grab look like rivets.

I made four gusseted side angle braces from Period Miniatures no. 2037 porch railings without posts. I started by slicing the top rail in half with a no. 11 blade so it has a thinner profile. I sliced down from the base of the railing at a 45-degree angle through the posts. Use cyanoacrylate adhesive (CA) to glue the angled braces in the second side panel in from each end, **7**.

Then I trimmed off the upper half of an Athearn Mill Gondola brake-wheel housing and glued a strip of .010" x .010" styrene to the housing to make a pump handle, attaching it to the left corner of the end of the car. I made the Apex Tri-Lok metal brake step from a 1 x 3-foot strip of a Micro-Trains running board that I filed down to a thin profile. I glued it to the top of the end sill below the Equipco brake housing, **8**.

To finish off the detailing of the gondola, I applied strips of Archer Fine Transfers N scale no. AR88024 resin rivet head decals along the floor line of the sides, **9**. I placed a single strip across the entire length of the car, and used Micro Set decal setting solution to get the strip into a perfectly straight row. The setting solution helps the decals fit over the side ribs. After the decals dried, I went back and cut out the rivets from the places where they overlapped the side ribs.

The end support for the auto frames is a permanent fixture in the car, **10**. I glued two scale 10-foot-long pieces of Evergreen .060" angle strip styrene a scale 12" in from the A end of the gondola. A 9-foot piece of angle styrene connects the two upright pieces across the top. I braced the upright supports with pieces of .015" x .015" styrene cut at 45-degree angles.

Painting

I airbrushed the car with a 1:1 mix of engine black and weathered black, followed by a topcoat of clear gloss to make it easier to apply the decals. I painted the interior of the car with roof brown and rust. These faded colors provided a nice contrast to the shiny new appearance of the auto frames.

I tend to reposition decals many times while they are wet before I get them perfectly aligned. Since dry transfers don't allow for repositioning, I turned them into decals by first applying them to a sheet of clear decal film. I sealed the transfers to the decal film with a spray of clear gloss.

I applied the PM decals and randomly placed several Clover House no. 9911-01 chalk marks on the car. I selected the smaller marks from this HO scale set, and scratched them a little bit to make them look slightly faded.

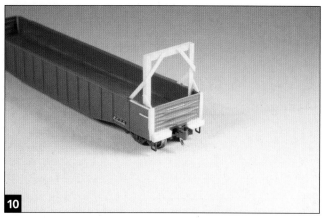

10

The auto frame rack is made from styrene and glued directly into the car.

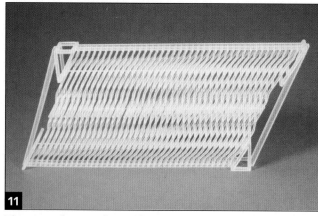

11

The auto frames from Shapeways are printed as a single piece. Clean them before separating the halves.

Then I sprayed the car with Testor's Dullcote, followed by light oversprays of thinned roof brown, rust, mud, and dust to give it a weathered look. I finished by dusting light powdered chalks dusted along the car to highlight the details along the sides and ends of the car.

Auto frame load

The load is built from a 3D printed part, Auto Frames for Gondola–N scale, available through Shapeways.com. The frames are printed in Frosted Ultra Detail, a matte translucent plastic. This is a perfect application of 3D printing technology for model railroading purposes. The parts beautifully capture the delicate curvature of the frames, which are printed in two interwoven rows, **11**. Each individual frame is interconnected with the ones beside it. The load has

stability, while allowing light to pass between the frames, perfectly capturing the look of a prototype auto frame load.

These particular parts are difficult to clean. I soaked them for three hours in Bestine solvent to melt the wax covering the parts. I sanded as much of the outer surfaces as I could safely reach, but the parts are small and delicate, so I could not reach all surfaces. However, in the end, this did not matter much because the parts are painted black and any remaining rough surfaces cannot be seen.

I designed this load to be removable, but it could also be glued permanently inside the gondola. Cut a piece of .020" sheet brass 3.335" x .660" to form the base of the load. The weight of the brass compensates for the weight lost in cutting away part of the underframe of the gondola.

Using CA, I glued a 43-foot piece of .060" x .060" styrene along the top outside edge of the brass weight, **12**. The strip extends 4'-6" beyond the base toward the gondola's end support.

I test-fit the parts and then glued the first stack of frames to the base. Make sure the end frame rests on the gondola's end support. I glued a 40-foot strip of .060" x .188" styrene down the center of the weight and then attached the second row of frames next to it. To finish the load, I glued a final 43-foot piece of .060" x .060" styrene along the top outside edge of the brass weight, **13**.

Next, I drilled a no. 76 hole in each base support strip, 8 feet back from the tie-down clamps. Drill the holes at a 45-degree angle, connecting the upper corner of the tie-down clamp with the base support strip. I inserted 9'-6"

Materials

Archer Fine Transfers
AR88024, N scale resin rivets

Athearn
Mill gondola rake wheel housing

Atlas Model Railroad
Trucks, 70-ton Hart ballast car

C-D-S Lettering dry transfers
N-794, Pere Marquette offset-side triple hoppers

Clover House dry transfers
9911-01, Chalk marks

Evergreen
HO scale styrene 4 x 6, 4 x 12, 6 x 12
291, Angle, .060"
Styrene, .010" x .010"
Styrene, .015" x .015"
Styrene, .030" x .060"
Styrene, .030" x .080"
Styrene, .060" x .060"
Styrene, .060" x .188"

Fox Valley Models
FVM-3302, Small flange wheelsets

Micro-Trains
1025, Couplers

1099, Gondola drop ends
10600200, 50-foot steel-side, 15-panel, fixed-end gondola

Period Miniatures
2037, Porch railings (no posts)

Shapeways (shapeways.com)
Auto frames, N scale

Miscellaneous
.015" diameter wire
.020" sheet brass
Clear decal film

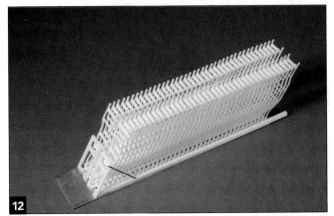

12 The frames and styrene supports are glued to the brass floor weight. Wire braces connect the frames to the supports.

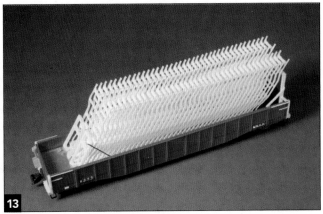

13 The load is designed to be removable, but it can be glued in permanently. Test-fit the auto frames before gluing everything down. The last frame should rest on the end support.

14 The gondola is purposely weathered and faded to provide a contrast to the freshly painted auto frames.

pieces of .015" wire into the holes and glued the upper ends of the wires to the sides of the tie-down clamps.

To finish, I airbrushed the loaded frames with CSX black, a shiny, dark paint that made the frames really stand out, 14. Use a bright light to inspect your paint job to make sure that every surface has been covered.

I used a fine detail brush to paint the tie-down clamps and wire supports with a mix of weathered black and engine black. Then I painted the exposed parts of the floor with a mix of roof brown and rust.

This gondola and its 3D printed load represent an iconic freight car from the golden age of the automobile.

Updating a former Railgon gondola

By Jeff Wilson

1

Gondolas are the most beat-up car type in the real world, so make sure your models represent it. Some weathering and a new load have aged this HO model considerably, making it look like it's earning its keep.

Railgon was formed in 1979 by parent Trailer Train Co. to provide a nationwide pool of gondolas for member railroads—much like Railbox had done in the early 1970s for boxcars. A total of 4,500 52-foot mill gondolas were in service by 1980.

However, railroad deregulation and other factors made these cars surplus within just a few years, **1**. Several individual railroads purchased these cars in the early 1980s, including Baltimore & Ohio, which bought 1,000 of them. The prototype car shows how the original RGON reporting marks were painted over and new lettering added, **2**.

Roundhouse (Model Die Casting, now owned by Athearn) once offered an inexpensive plastic HO scale kit for the car. I had built one several years ago, and it's the subject of this project. Athearn currently offers an upgraded ready-to-run version of this car, including separate grab irons and metal wheels. I decided to upgrade my original, doing my best to duplicate the general wear and tear shown on the prototype car.

2

This Railgon car had been in service 13 years in this 1992 photo, but it looks older with its missing and worn lettering, new reporting marks and capacity data, and lots of rust and general wear and tear.

Body details

I added some basic underframe details, including a Cal-Scale brake set (this is, of course, optional), **3**. As the photo shows, some brake gear and rods are visible under the car. This car has vertically mounted levers at each end. I cut levers from .010" styrene and glued them to the center sill. Next, I added the cylinder, control valve, and reservoir as the photo shows. The rods and pipes are .012" brass wire, bent to shape and inserted in no. 80 holes drilled in each of the components. This is meant to convey the basic appearance of brake gear and not replicate each item from the real car. I then brush-painted everything black.

Since I use manual uncoupling tools, I usually choose to cut the steel uncoupling pins from couplers for improved realism (don't do this if you use magnetic uncouplers). I did this with the Kadee couplers and installed them at each end, **4**. Glue a Cal-Scale hose mounting bracket and hose next to each coupler. Follow this with a wire eye bolt and Detail Associates uncoupling lever at each end.

I wanted to upgrade the brake wheel on the end of the car, so I shaved off the existing housing, **5**. You can use a chisel-tip hobby knife blade for this, but I prefer Micro-Mark's detail-removing chisel. It provides a strong cutting edge and more control, and it leaves a very clean surface when you're done.

Glue the new brake housing in place from the Cal-Scale set, **6**. Then glue the new Kadee modern brake wheel in

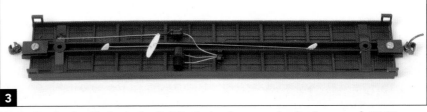

3

Underbody details include Cal-Scale brake gear, brake levers of .010" styrene, and .012" brass rods as pipe and levers.

place on the Cal-Scale housing, painting it if necessary. (I had a red one handy, so I simply painted it black.)

I used the car's simulated modern roller-bearing truck sideframes, but swapped new metal 36" smooth-back wheelsets in place of the model's original plastic wheels.

Weathering

A large part of the appeal of this car is its beat-up, weathered appearance, with lots of rust showing and much of the original lettering fading from view. I used a pencil eraser to remove much of the factory-applied lettering, adding a bit of Solvaset decal solution to speed

the process, **7**. I removed all of the original GONX and other lettering to replicate the prototype car.

If you're doing this on another car, depending upon what the manufacturer uses for lettering (most use ink instead of paint), you may have to use fine sandpaper or the tip of a hobby knife to remove the lettering.

I found the B&O reporting marks lettering in a Microscale N scale set (no. 60-55), but you could also use an alphabet set as well. I applied the reporting marks and then added some chalk scribbling from another Microscale set (Sunshine and Clover House both offer chalk mark sets), **8**.

Materials

Athearn/Model Die Casting
Railgon kit or ready-to-run car

Cal Scale
190-283, Brake set

Chooch
7225, Cast-resin scrap load

Detail Associates
2206, Wire eye bolts
2504, .012" brass wire
6215, Uncoupling levers

Kadee
5, Couplers
522, 36" metal wheelsets
2045, Brake wheel (modern black)

4 The Kadee coupler fits in the Roundhouse coupler pocket. The uncoupling pin is cut off, while a brake hose and uncoupling lever have been added.

5 Cut off the original brake housing with a hobby knife or Micro-Mark chisel (shown).

6 Glue the new Cal-Scale brake housing in place above the molded brake platform. Then add the Kadee brake wheel.

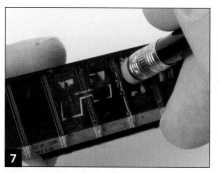

7 Erase much of the factory-applied lettering with a pencil eraser. Wetting the area with Solvaset speeds the process.

8 Add the new reporting mark decals above the car number.

9 Roof brown paint and artist's tube acrylics work well for simulating rust patches, worn lettering, and rusty areas.

I goofed a bit with my model—I realized later that the model's number is not in the series of cars purchased by the B&O sequence (nos. 350000–350999). I figured the car is weathered heavily enough that it would take a hardcore B&O fan to notice my mistake.

Prototype cars are periodically reweighed, with new data stenciled in place of the old. In the case of this prototype, this was done by painting out the original light weight and load limit with boxcar red paint and then adding new data with white stencils. Duplicate this in the same way: paint out the original data with red paint and use some decal or dry transfer lettering to add new numbers (I found some in my decal scrapbox). I wasn't particular about the specific numbers because they will be weathered later.

You can now weather the car with any number of techniques. I painted some rust areas over old lettering with roof brown paint, **9**. I then added some rust patches with that as well as acrylic

artist's (tube) paints: burnt sienna for brighter rust and raw umber for darker areas. Tube acrylics work well because they provide some texture as well as color.

I gave the car a light overspray of a thinned mix of black and grimy black paint. I then used black and dark gray chalks to streak down the car sides. When I was done, I finished with a light overspray of clear flat finish. (I used Model Master clear acryl applied with an airbrush; you can use your preferred clear coat from a can or airbrush.)

Load

Decide if you want to include a load in the car. My car was originally empty, so I had weathered the interior with washes of rust-color paint (see the Pere Marquette car on pages 69–70 for ideas) followed by brown and orange powdered chalk. Later, I decided to add one of Chooch's excellent cast-resin simulated scrap loads. I used various

10 Cut the load to fit. Styrene spacers elevate the load to the proper height. Glue the spacers to the load, not the car.

shades of dark brown paint to highlight individual elements in the load.

Cut the load to fit with a razor saw if needed (wear a dust mask, as resin dust is a major lung irritant). I test-fit the load by resting it on a couple of scrap styrene pieces in each end of the car to get the load to a level just below the car top, **10**. Glue the styrene pieces to the load and set the load in the car—this allows you to remove the load at any time for photos or operations.

Building a 3D printed PRR gondola

By Keith Kohlmann

1

The finished N scale Shapeways 3D printed Pennsy GR gondola with Micro-Trains trucks and couplers carries a removable limestone load.

I wanted to build an N scale model of a version of the Pennsylvania Railroad's GR class gondola as they appeared in the early 1950s, 1. These were old cars by then, having been built by the Pressed Steel Car Co. beginning in 1902.

The gondola was a common car. By February 1920, there were 16,200 GR class gondolas in service. Half of these were still in service into 1947, and approximately 200 remained by 1953, with many retired cars placed in nonrevenue service. GR gondolas could be found in maintenance-of-way trains

well into the Conrail era. The Long Island Rail Road also used these cars.

The cars were designed for hauling long structural steel material. The 50-ton capacity cars were equipped with drop ends and all-steel underframes that featured deep side sills and fish-belly center beams.

The sidewalls were 3½"-thick wood planks bolted to permanent steel side supports. The sides were only used to contain the load and were not part of the structural support system. Side stake pockets were part of the original design, which allowed for temporary

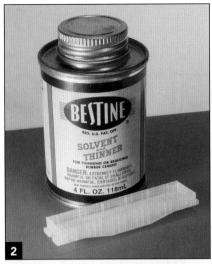

2 Soak the Shapeways 3D printed model in Bestine or Simple Green to melt off the support wax residue.

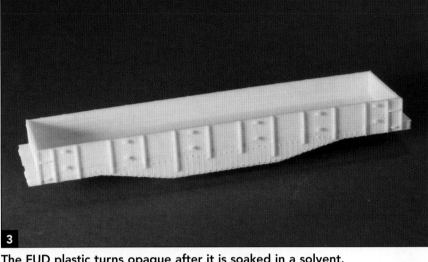

3 The FUD plastic turns opaque after it is soaked in a solvent.

extensions to the sides of the cars. The stake pockets were removed when the cars were refurbished in the late 1930s as part of an effort to smooth out the sides.

Challenge

Even with styrene construction techniques, this unique car was going to be a challenge to build in N scale. This changed with the advent of 3D printing, along with Archer Fine Transfers raised decal rivets. Shapeways (shapeways.com) is an online 3D printing service that accepts model design files from users. Printed versions of these models (in several scales) can be ordered through the website. The models arrive ready to clean up, modify, and paint. This is an exciting new technology that allows designers to share their models of specific prototypes that would otherwise not be economical to mass-produce.

Building a 3D printed model is an interesting adventure that combines traditional modeling techniques with a new medium. I ordered the N scale PRR GR class gondola that was printed in Frosted Ultra Detail (FUD), which is a matte translucent plastic material. Due to the nature of 3D printing, not all small details can be produced in N scale. Trucks, couplers, and weight must also be added to the gondola.

Construction

The 3D printed model is covered in wax support material during the printing process. This wax is partially removed before the model is shipped. Straight from the package, FUD appears to be a frosted translucent plastic. Before any work can take place on the model, you must remove the remaining wax, **2**.

To do so, place the model in a small metal pan filled with Bestine Solvent and Thinner (Simple Green Industrial Cleaner & Degreaser makes a good alternative). I sealed the pan inside a plastic bag to keep the fumes from filling up the room. The solvent melted the wax after about four hours. After that time, I scrubbed the model gently with a soft toothbrush to remove stubborn waxy areas. The model now appeared as dull white opaque plastic, **3**. I washed the model with dish soap and warm water and set it aside to dry. Be careful not to break off any small detail parts in the process of cleaning it.

A rough, patterned texture is an unfortunate effect of 3D printing that appears in the surface of the car. It is most noticeable on the smooth "steel" surfaces on the frame. To eliminate this condition, you can sand, scrape, or file the sides smooth. This will wipe out the rivet detailing, but you can put that back on the car with Archer rivets once the sides are smooth. Get all parts of the car as smooth as possible

before moving on to the detailing and assembly steps.

This lightweight car will not run properly without adding some weight. Unfortunately, no provision was made for hiding weights, but adequate space can be made beneath the car, **4**. I began by grinding away all the underside detailing between the bolsters with a router bit in a motor tool, **5**.

The National Model Railroad Association recommended weight for a 40-foot car is 1.1 ounces. To achieve this, I stacked three pieces of .030"-thick brass sheet underneath the car. Each piece is .635" wide, and the three pieces are 1.5", 1.4", and .765" long. I test-fit the brass weights to make sure they would be hidden when centered under the car, and then glued them in place with cyanoacrylate adhesive (CA), **6**.

I filed down the bolsters to match the bottom edge of the side sills. I deepened the truck-mounting hole in each bolster with a ¹⁄₁₆" drill bit, and then test-fit Micro-Trains no. 1001-B brown Bettendorf trucks. I replaced the original plastic wheelsets with Fox Valley Models FVM-3302 small-flange metal wheelsets.

The floor is not thick enough to support a screw for the coupler box, so I added some supporting styrene, **7** and **8**. I cut two pieces of .030" sheet to .400" x .640" and glued them inside the car with CA.

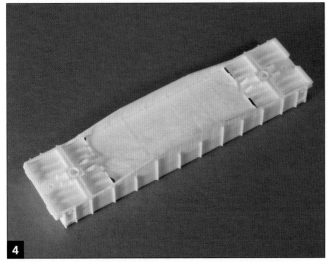

4 Create a flat space for the brass weights needed to make the car run properly.

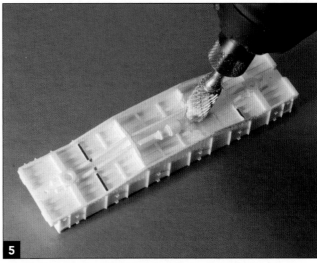

5 Carefully grind out the underframe detailing with a grinding bit in a rotary tool.

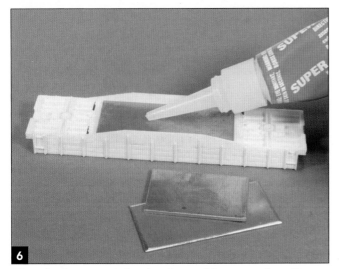

6 Glue the brass weights in place with super glue. Keep the weights hidden behind the sideframes.

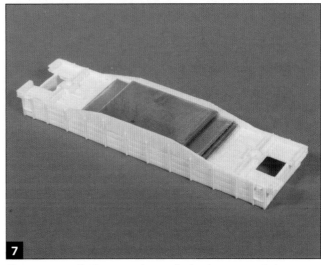

7 Cut spaces all the way through the bottom of the car for the coupler pockets.

I also added a pair of Micro-Trains no. 1025 couplers. I drilled the mounting holes for the couplers with a no. 62 bit, and then used a no. 00-90 screw and a small dab of Walthers Goo to mount the couplers. The plastic is soft enough that the screws can be self-tapping. The glue will keep the coupler box from rotating out of position when the car goes around sharp curves.

Next, I used a razor saw to make small cuts at each corner in the ends of the body to hold the corner stirrups, **9**. I cut the stirrups from a set of Micro-Trains no. 1079 gondola stirrups. I inserted the upper backing support into the saw kerf at each corner, and glued them in place with CA.

To represent the support braces added when the cars were rebuilt, I glued short strips of .010" x .030" styrene between the two outermost panels.

I drilled two holes in the B (brake) end of the car with a no. 62 bit to mount a Micro-Trains vertical brake wheel, **10**. I test-fit the brake wheel, but didn't glue it in place with CA until all the painting, decaling, and weathering was done. If you are building this car in the "as-built" condition, it was originally constructed with a brake wheel at each end. (The February 1990 *Mainline Modeler* includes details.)

Finishing
Archer uses 3D printing to place rows of resin dots on decal paper to represent scale-sized rivets. These strips are cut from the sheet and applied just like normal decals. Using prototype photos for reference, I placed strips of rivets from set AR 88028 on the car. When painted, the heads stick up through the paint for a very realistic appearance.

I painted the entire car with a primer coat of light gray, followed by a layer of oxide red with a dusting of roof brown, **11**. After letting the car dry completely, I inspected the finish for places where more sanding or rivets were needed. I repaired those locations and covered them with more oxide red paint and some roof brown shadowing. A topcoat of clear gloss helped hide the decal film.

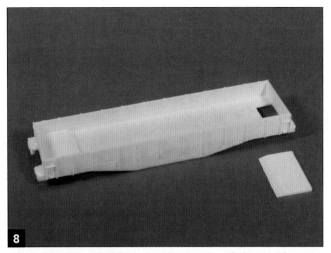

8 Glue a styrene platform to the inside of the car for attaching the couplers.

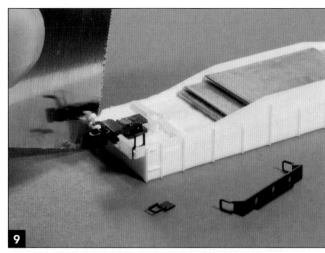

9 Saw a notch at each corner to accept the stirrup steps.

10 Mount a Micro-Trains brake wheel to the end of the car.

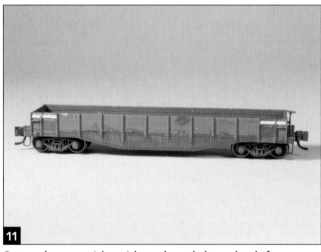

11 Spray the car with oxide red, and then check for areas that need to be sanded more.

I applied decals from Microscale set no. 60-1510 Pennsylvania early freight cars. When they dried, I sealed them with a coat of Testor's Dullcote. To finish, I airbrushed light, thinned coats of mud and dust to the car's lower parts.

I made a limestone load by trimming an old Trix hopper car coal load insert to fit inside the gondola. I painted the insert light gray, then covered it with matte medium, and sprinkled white limestone ballast into

the wet glue. After the glue dried completely, I filed the rough stone-covered edges smooth so the insert fit easily inside the car. You can do the same with a plain piece of plastic cut to fit the car opening.

Materials

Shapeways (shapeways.com)
N scale PRR GR Class Gondola, printed in Frosted Ultra Detail

Archer Fine Transfers
AR88028, Resin rivets

Fox Valley Models
FVM-3302, Small-flange metal wheelsets

Micro-Trains
1001-B, Brown Bettendorf trucks
1025, Couplers
1079, Gondola stirrups
1089, Vertical brakewheel

Microscale decals
60-1510, Pennsylvania Early Freight Cars

Miscellaneous
Brass sheet, .030" thick
Styrene sheet, .030"
Styrene, .010" x030"

Adding a pipe load to a mill gondola

By Jeff Wilson

1

Pipe loads are common on real trains, and make for interesting model loads. Making a load is easy and economical using soda straws.

Pipe loads are common in gondolas, and modeling one is a relatively easy and inexpensive project. I had an HO Proto 2000 gondola handy, and the car style matched a B&O gondola. I decided to give it a pipe load for my mid-1960s-era layout, **1**.

Pipe comes in many diameters, lengths, materials, and colors. Light-gauge steel pipe is usually stacked and banded together, but some types of pipe include wood spacing blocks between each layer. I decided to keep it fairly simple and build a load like that on the B&O car, **2**.

Body preparation

My model was lettered for Pere Marquette, but the road name doesn't really matter for this project. Mill gons see a lot of abuse, and even cars that are only a few years old show lots of scrapes, dents, rust, and worn paint and lettering. This one would be about 20 years old for the time I'm modeling, so I weathered it heavily.

I started by applying washes of artist's (tube) oil colors on both the interior and exterior surfaces, **3**. I used four colors: Mars black (to fade the lettering), raw sienna (light rust), burnt sienna (darker rust), and burnt umber

2 The pipe load in this Baltimore & Ohio mill gondola is stacked, held together with bands, and kept in place in the car by vertical posts. *Trains magazine collection*

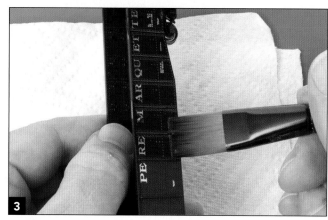

3 Weather the car with washes of rust-colored artist's oil paints, brushing them downward along each side panel.

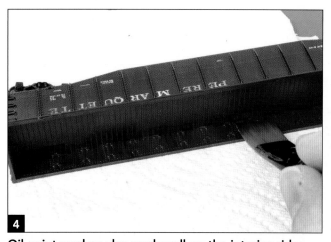

4 Oil paint washes also work well on the interior sides and floor.

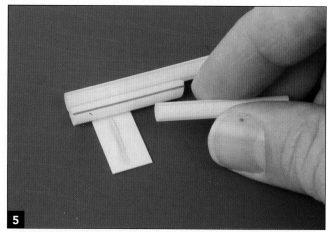

5 Glue the first layer of straws to a styrene base using E-6000 adhesive. I recommend a long styrene base instead of the short ones I initially used.

(dark rust). To do this, squeeze a bit of each color (it doesn't take much) on a plain card or aluminum artist's palette. Then dip a wide brush in turpentine, touch it to one or more of the colors, and stroke the brush down the car side.

The turpentine/oil wash takes longer to dry than acrylics do, giving you plenty of working time to get the effects the way you want. If a wash appears too dark, use a clean brush of turpentine to thin it and redo the effect.

A variation of this step is to paint rust patches on the surface with oil colors. Let them dry and then wash a brush of turpentine across it and down the car side a couple of times. This results in a rust streak that is heavy directly below the rust patch and lighter down the side.

I did the same thing to the car interior, using various rust colors on both

the interior sides and floor, **4**. I also gave the trucks a rust wash and painted the wheel faces dark brown with black highlights.

Let the car dry a day or two and then seal the effects with a coat of clear flat or semigloss. You can then add additional weathering (more washes, chalk, or any other effect) if you wish. Seal each layer of weathering with a clear coat.

Pipe load

Disposable plastic straws of various sizes can be used to represent pipe loads. The first step is to cut the straws to length. I used scissors to cut mine a scale 50 feet long, which seemed appropriate, and ensured that they'd fit in the car's 52-foot-long interior.

If you have enough of them, you can simply build the entire stack with

whole straws. I didn't have enough straws on hand (and I didn't want to run to a store just to try and find matching straws), so I cheated by using some short lengths on each end, making the stack hollow in the middle.

Figure out how wide the load can be—this will vary based on your straws and the model that you're using. The inside width of this car is a scale 9 feet, and I needed to allow room for 4 x 4 wood stakes along each side. Five straws side-by-side worked out almost perfectly for the straws I had, so I decided to make my load a series of alternating layers of five straws with four straws.

To keep the bottom layer flat, I glued each end of a straw to a small piece of styrene slightly narrower than the load. I would instead recommend using a long piece of styrene as a base

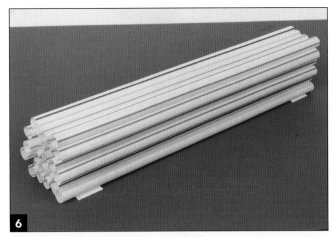

6 This stack is complete and ready for painting. You'd never know the stack is hollow from the outside.

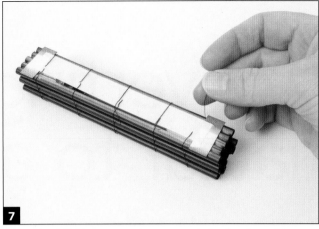

7 Glue the EZ Line strapping around the load, making sure the spacing is relatively even.

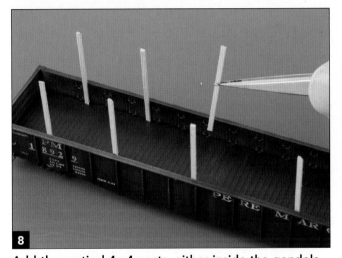

8 Add the vertical 4 x 4 posts, either inside the gondola as shown or by gluing them directly to the load.

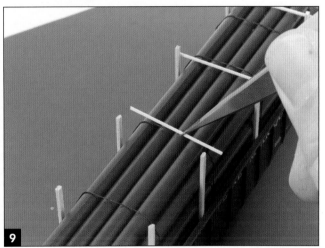

9 Glue lengths of scale 2 x 3 stripwood across the posts above the load.

(you can see I added one later)—it makes gluing and aligning the straws and straps easier.

Glue the straws to the styrene base and to each other with E-6000 adhesive, **5**. This is a clear, flexible, strong adhesive that works well for slippery plastic surfaces like these. Build up the layers of straws, being careful to keep the adhesive on the inside and bottom surfaces of the straws so the adhesive isn't visible. Test-fit the load in the car after the first layer is in place to make sure it fits properly and then again when the stack is complete, **6**.

Paint the finished stack of straws with an airbrush or spray can. I used an airbrush and Modelflex roof brown, but pipes come in many colors, so feel free to improvise or follow a prototype car.

Prototype stacks are secured by several straps surrounding the load. I

used five pieces of Berkshire Junction EZ Line, an elastic thread. Use super glue to fix one end of each thread to the styrene base, spacing them evenly along the load. Pull each line around the load, keeping it aligned, and glue the free end in place, **7**.

You can make the load removable by gluing the 4 x 4 posts to the load itself (be very sparing with adhesive, and keep the glue below the level of the top of the sides if possible). I simply glued the posts to the inside of the gondola with cyanoacrylate adhesive (CA), keeping the spacing even on both sides, and then set the load in place, **8**. In photo **2**, you can see that the posts in the prototype car have shifted quite a bit, but my posts are vertical.

The vertical posts are typically tied together over the top of the load either

with cable (as in the prototype photo) or with boards. I used CA to glue cross pieces of scale 2 x 3 stripwood to the posts (two for each pair of posts, one on each side), **9**. You can use EZ Line to simulate wire if you desire.

Materials

Proto 2000 (Walthers)
54120, Mill gondola, Pere Marquette

Midwest Products stripwood
8001, HO 2 x 3
8016, HO 4 x 4

Miscellaneous
Soda straws
Berkshire Junction EZ Line (black)

Converting a BN flatcar to a gondola

By Cody Grivno

1

Burlington Northern no. 621549, a bulkhead flatcar turned gondola, waits to be loaded at the scrapyard. This project came about after I saw the prototype car while driving to work.

One of the benefits of my drive to work is that I cross three different railroads. Is it the most direct route? No (please don't tell my boss). However, it does put a variety of modeling ideas right in front of my camera's viewfinder. It was during one of my commutes that I came across Burlington Northern no. 621549, **1**. The former bulkhead flatcar had been converted to a gondola and was hauling scrap wheels the day I saw it, **2**. The unique car begged to be modeled, which didn't take much convincing

since it was painted Cascade Green. As you may have guessed, I'm a BN fan.

I used an Athearn Ready-to-Roll car as the starting point for this project, **3**. It's not an exact match for the prototype, as the stake pocket locations and some of the details are a bit different. However, once the sides are added and the car is weathered, it makes a plausible stand-in.

Making the sides

The Athearn model has 13 stake pockets, while the prototype has 15. To match the prototype, on the model,

I cut notches in the first full board closest to the bulkhead to make room for new pockets. I goofed up my first attempt at this car, so I cut stake pockets off the damaged car and attached them to a second car, **4**. If you don't have a second car, you could fashion new stake pockets from styrene.

Next, I made the sides. First, I cut two 7²³⁄₃₂" pieces of .030" styrene sheet. Then I added ⁵⁄₁₆" lengths of ¹⁄₁₆" styrene I beams, spaced to match the stake pockets. (I cut the end stakes slightly shorter, as the new stake pockets aren't as deep as the factory pockets.) I made the cap strip from .015" x .100" styrene strip, **5**. I used styrene-compatible glue to assemble the parts.

I then spray-painted the sides with Rust-Oleum Painter's Touch 2X flat red primer, **6**. This paint is plastic compatible, so it won't craze the styrene. The color also makes a great base for simulating rusty metal.

2 This prototype photo won't win style points for quality, but its subject sparked a unique modeling project.

Quick relettering

As with my other projects in this book, I used Micro Sol to remove the lettering. After brushing the decal-setting solution on the model and letting it evaporate, I was able to scrape away the white lettering with a round-head toothpick, **7**. Once all of the lettering was removed, I wet-sanded the sides and end plates with 1,500-grit sandpaper, being careful not to remove the Cascade Green paint.

Then I washed the model in warm water and dish soap to remove

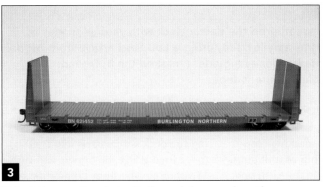

3 This Athearn Ready-to-Roll model served as the starting point for this project.

4 The model needed two extra stake pockets per side. I cut notches in the first full board closest to the bulkhead for the new pockets. I used pockets from a car I damaged in my first attempt at modeling the 621549.

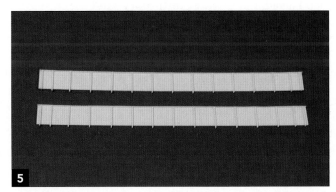

5 I made the new walls using assorted styrene sheet and strip. The sides (.030" sheet) and cap (.015" x .100" strip) measure 7²³⁄₃₂". The posts (¹⁄₁₆" I beam) are ⁵⁄₁₆" tall, except for the ones closest to the bulkhead on each end.

6 After assembling the sides, I spray-painted them with Rust-Oleum Painter's Touch 2X flat red primer. This plastic-compatible paint provides a great base for simulating rusty metal.

7 I applied Micro Sol over the factory printing. Once the decal-setting solution evaporated, I gently scraped away the lettering with a round-head toothpick.

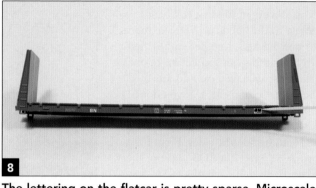

8 The lettering on the flatcar is pretty sparse. Microscale set 87-1381 completed most of the car. The Clean, Oil, Test & Stencil panel is from set MC-5004.

9 The last decals to be applied were the side road numbers. At this point, the clean Cascade Green paint behind the number is hard to see. This will change once the subsequent weathering is added.

10 I weathered the flatcar deck with various shades of gray acrylic paint, using a Lou Sassi article from *Model Railroader* as a guide. I masked the bulkheads with blue painter's tape.

the white paint flecks that stuck to the model and any impurities that might affect paint adhesion. Then I sprayed the model with two coats of Model Master gloss clear to provide a smooth, shiny surface for decal application.

I let the gloss clear dry for 24 hours before applying decals from Microscale set 87-1381, **8**. The side road numbers on the full-size car appear to have been reapplied, as there is fresh paint beneath them. I left those off the model for now.

After wiping the model with distilled water to remove any residue from the decaling process, I sprayed the car with a thin coat of gloss clear to seal the decals. Once that had dried, I masked off the area where the side road numbers would go. Then I sprayed the car with thinned Model Master reefer white and leather (1 part paint to 9 parts 70 percent isopropyl alcohol). The reefer white gives the green a faded look, while the leather

gives the lettering a slightly rusty appearance. With the weathering completed, I removed the masking tape and applied another thin coat of gloss clear to protect the initial weathering.

Next, I applied the side road numbers, **9**. As before, I sealed these decals with a thin coat of gloss clear. I thinned the gloss clear 50:50 with 70 percent isopropyl alcohol. Though I already applied several layers of gloss clear, it didn't look too thick because it was heavily thinned.

Hit the deck
The basis for the deck weathering technique is Lou Sassi's article "Weathering a flatcar in one evening" from the June 2009 issue of *Model Railroader*. I masked the lower portion of the bulkheads, and then brush-painted the entire deck with Model Master reefer gray. I followed that by brush-painting individual boards with Polly Scale D&H gray and new gravel gray, **10**.

After the paint had dried, I switched gears. Instead of weathering the deck with pastels like Lou did, I used greige, tie brown, and rust Weathering Mix from Hunterline. Though these alcohol-based stains are designed for wood, they worked well on this plastic car, **11**.

Rust and more rust
Whether it's a conventional gondola or a modified car like BN no. 621549, cars in scrap service don't stay shiny and new for long. One thing that really stood out in the prototype photos was the scrapes and dings on the bulkheads. Pelle Søeborg wrote about a weathering paste to simulate rust patches in his book *Detailing Projects for Freight Cars & Locomotives* (Kalmbach, 2013). Using this as inspiration, I mixed A.I.M. Products dark rust, grimy black, and light rust weathering powders with Acrylicos Vallejo matte varnish.

Pelle applied his paste with a fine brush, which looks great on his models

11

Instead of weathering the gray with pastels like Lou did, I used alcohol-based Weathering Mix from Hunterline. The colors used here are greige, tie brown, and rust.

12

I made a weathering paste by mixing A.I.M. weathering powders with Acrylicos Vallejo matte varnish. I created realistic scratches on the bulkheads by applying the weathering paste with .015" brass rod.

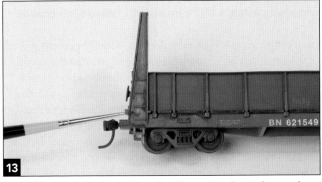

13

I used paints designed to simulate weathered wood to add rust patches. The lighter color suggests fresh rust, while the darker color re-creates the look of aged rust. The vertical streaks of light gray mimic the look of oxidized paint.

14

Colored pencils aren't just for art class. I used Prismacolor pencils to add graffiti to the car. I brush-painted Burlington Northern green on the I beams based on prototype photos.

but that didn't create the look I was after here. In a stroke of late-night desperation, I applied the paste with a .015" brass rod. As you can see in photo **12**, I worked in a random pattern. In some cases, I dragged the rod through the fresh paste and created prototypical battle scars.

I used a paintbrush to apply the paste at the base of the bulkheads, where the loads would be in regular contact with the car. In addition, I drybrushed the rust-colored paste on the bulkheads, sides, and ends.

Then, using prototype photos as a guide, I added heavier rust patches to the sides and ends of the car. On the full-size car, there is quite a bit of rust above the trucks and on the sides of the bulkheads. To re-create that look, I used Lifecolor UA 713 warm dark shade and UA 714 warm base color from the company's Weathered Wood set. But wait, isn't this a steel car? Yes,

it is. But the wood weathering colors do a great job of simulating rust.

Using an 18/0 spotter brush, I first applied patches of warm base color, which looks like fresh rust. Though the application may look random, it's not entirely. Rust typically forms along edges and weld seams, around nut-bolt-washer castings, and above ladder rungs where the paint is worn off by employees getting on and off the car during switching moves.

Once the warm base color dried, I applied the warm dark shade in the center of the patches, **13**. This color is a good approximation for rust that has been on the car for a while.

After applying the rust patches, I randomly drybrushed streaks of Model Master camouflage gray to simulate oxidized paint. Keep the brush parallel to the bulkheads and car sides when drybrushing, otherwise it will ruin the effect.

Finishing touches

I did a bit more work on the car sides before installing them. First, I mixed up a new batch of rust paste and weathered the backs using the same techniques I used on the bulkheads. After the weathering paste had dried, I applied Hunterline rust and tie brown Weathering Mix with a paintbrush.

Then I flipped the sides over and used an airbrush to apply thinned grimy black (1 part paint to 9 parts 70 percent isopropyl alcohol) under the cap strips and along the I beams. I then sprayed the panels with oxide red, thinned to the same ratio. This technique creates a realistic mix of shadows and highlights. I sealed the weathering by spraying the sides with Model Master flat clear.

I test-fit the sides prior to installation. The paint added a bit of thickness to the styrene, so I used a single-edge razor blade to shave off some of the

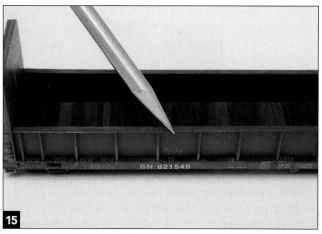

15 To simulate the look of worn metal, I rubbed a metallic silver color pencil along the edges of the cap strips.

16 I airbrushed the truck sideframes grimy black and brush-painted the springs leather. I painted the metal wheelsets using a Microbrush and railroad tie brown.

paint and styrene. Then I secured the sides with Plastruct Bondene.

The prototype car has graffiti on the sides, which I simulated with Prismacolor Verithin tuscan red and white colored pencils, **14**. Then, following prototype photos, I used an 18/0 paintbrush to apply Burlington Northern green to select I beams.

I again turned to colored pencils, this time metallic silver, to create the look of worn metal. I rubbed the pencil along the edges of the cap strips, areas that would likely be hit when the car is loaded and unloaded, **15**. A little of this goes a long way, so don't overdo it.

To give the model a uniform finish, I used an airbrush to spray the car with two coats of flat clear.

Finally, I masked the sockets and sprayed the truck sideframes grimy black, **16**. I brush-painted the springs leather, a surprisingly good rust color, so they'd stand out. Then I cleaned the metal wheelsets with 70 percent isopropyl alcohol and painted them with a Microbrush and railroad tie brown. I weathered the couplers using the same techniques explained in "Upgrading a basic covered hopper" on pages 51–52.

Real railroads, like modelers, have to improvise on occasion, as this bulkhead flatcar turned gondola illustrates. This unusual model is sure to draw attention, whether rolling in a manifest freight or waiting to get loaded at a scrapyard.

Materials

Acrylicos Vallejo
70.520, Matte varnish

A.I.M. Products weathering powders
3102, Grimy Black
3105, Dark Rust
3106, Light Rust

Athearn Trains
ATH87700, Burlington Northern 60-foot bulkhead flatcar

Evergreen
115, Styrene strip, .015" x .100"
9030, Styrene .030"

Hunterline weathering mix
Greige
Rust
Tie Brown

Lifecolor acrylic paint
CS 20, Weathered wood diorama set

Microscale
MC-5004, Clean, Oil, Test & Stencil triple panels, 1990+
104, Micro Set
105, Micro Sol
87-1381, Burlington Northern flatcars, bulkhead flatcars, and center-beam flatcars

Model Master acrylic paint
4636, Flat Clear
4638, Gloss Clear
4674, Leather
4766, Camouflage Gray
4873, Reefer White
4882, Oxide Red
4885, Railroad Tie Brown
4886, Reefer Gray
4887, Grimy Black

Plastruct styrene
90511, 1⁄16" I beam

Prismacolor Verithin colored pencils
734, White
746-1⁄2, Tuscan Red
753, Metallic Silver

Polly Scale
414197, D&H Gray
414209, Burlington Northern Green
414332, New Gravel Gray

Rust-Oleum
249086, Painter's Touch 2X Flat Red Primer

Building a realistic deck for a NP flatcar

By Mont Switzer

1

Using wood stir sticks for a deck gives this HO Northern Pacific flatcar a rough and realistic appearance.

I have been bringing wooden stir sticks home with me from every trip I've taken for the last 30 years. They were first used to stir my coffee and then when faced with the decision of whether to toss the stick or wrap it in a napkin for the trip home, I always chose the latter. The coffee stain only enhanced the stick's appearance. You can buy new wooden stir sticks at some grocery stores and wholesale food and office supply dealers.

I wanted to work with clean material free of any surface residue, so I dumped all the wooden sticks I had on hand into a pan of warm tap water with dishwashing detergent added. I swirled them around a bit, emptied the water, and placed the wooden stir sticks on paper towels to dry. Don't leave the wooden sticks in the water so long that they become waterlogged and risk becoming warped when they dry.

When the wooden sticks have dried, they need to be sorted. As with the prototype, the most important dimension is thickness; length is of secondary importance. I had stir sticks with thicknesses of .040" and .090". I stored each size in its own plastic bag with the

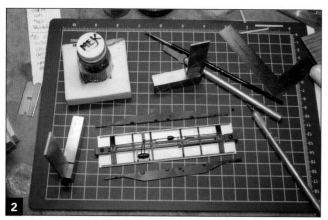

To begin replacing the kit's simulated wood floor panel, lay the floor panel on a larger styrene sheet and cut around it with a sharp hobby knife.

Cut the wooden stir sticks into sections the same width as the subfloor. The NorthWest Short Line Chopper makes short work of accurately cutting the stir sticks.

thickness of the wood clearly marked on the bag.

The next flatcar project to hit my workbench was the HO scale Central Valley Model Works 41-foot flatcar (kit no. 1003), which has a separate floor or deck section. It is modeled after a Depression era Northern Pacific prototype that was operated by subsequent owner Burlington Northern into the 1980s. Kit assembly was typical of today's well-detailed, molded styrene kits. Only basic hobby tools are required to achieve a nice model and the detailing is up to you. I decided to replace the model's deck and add some more realistic details, **1**.

Replacing the subfloor
To replace the molded styrene, simulated wood floor with a wood floor, I first cut a .010" sheet styrene subfloor to the exact size of the simulated wood floor panel from the kit, **2**. Simply lay the floor panel kit on a larger styrene sheet and cut around it with a sharp hobby knife or single-edge razor blade. Although I used Evergreen white styrene, I recommend using black styrene instead, so any cracks between flooring boards show as black.

Cutting sufficient material
Begin cutting the wooden stir sticks into sections the same width as the subfloor, **3**. To determine when you have enough stir stick sections to cover the subfloor, simply line them up on top of the subfloor until it is completely covered. Then cut several extras

just in case. I used a NorthWest Short Line Chopper to easily cut the stir sticks into consistent lengths.

Slice each wooden stir stick section lengthwise into two or three pieces, keeping the pieces as straight as possible, **4**. A single-edge razor blade is perfect for this task. There are many cuts to be made, so mounting the razor blade in a mini-scraper handle makes this task much easier on your fingers. The handle helps you place downward pressure on the blade. Your new boards will be a random width since it is impossible to cut them the same every time.

Once all the sections have been cut into two or three pieces, put them into a single container and shake the container until boards are thoroughly mixed. Then take them out and neatly stack them in a pile.

Floor installation
I began installing the new floorboards at each end of the car and worked toward the center, **5**. Select your boards at random from the pile one at a time, and install them on the styrene subfloor. Paint Elmer's Glue-All onto the subfloor a little at a time to keep the boards in place. Use a piece of 20-pound copy paper as a temporary spacer between the boards as you install them. Keep a machinist square handy to check your work periodically as you go. You want to keep the individual boards square on both ends as you install them. The last board in the center of the car floor has to be cut to

the correct width to fit the remaining opening unless you happen to have a board the right width. Turn the model over with the floor down, place a weight on it, and allow the glue to dry overnight.

The floor has a look all of its own that cannot be mistaken for a molded styrene simulated wood floor, **6**. If the edges of the wood flooring are a little uneven, smooth them out with a few strokes of a sanding block. To complete, the floor will need to be weathered.

Weathering the wood deck
To weather the flatcar's deck to resemble weathered oak, I used black acrylic paints thinned with Windex window cleaner. I dabbed a small amount of the paint paste on an inverted plastic container, which acts as a pallet. I then added Windex to the pallet. The Windex does not mix with the acrylic paint right away so dab your brush in the alcohol-rich window cleaner first and then touch it to the paint. Brush the paint mix onto the wood flooring, and as the wood soaks up the thinned coloring, it will turn light gray. If your first attempt leaves the floor too light, repeat the process. Between the irregular board spacing and the irregular coloring, there is a big difference between this wood flooring and the regularly spaced flooring.

Underbody
I added single Evergreen .030" x .040" styrene stringers (no. 132) along both

4 Use a single-edge razor blade to cut the stir sticks lengthwise into two or three pieces. Mounting the razor blade in a mini-scraper handle allows you to more easily make the cuts and provides a random width since to is almost impossible to cut them the same width.

5 Install the boards randomly on a sheet styrene subfloor, starting at the ends and working to the center. Use Elmer's Glue-All to keep the boards in place. Keep a machinist square handy to check your work as you go.

6 When compared to a molded styrene, simulated wood floor, the stir-stick floor looks more realistic. Weathering the floor is the next step.

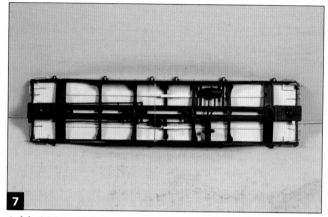

7 Add .030" x .040" styrene stringers along both sides of the underbody so they fit between the cross members. Then add wire grab irons and a .008" wire across the entire car and through both side sills to simulate the rod that operates the retainer valve.

sides of the underbody, **7**. The stringers must be cut to fit between the cross members. Cut each piece slightly oversize, lay them in place, and then trim to fit. When trimmed to the final size and in the final position, add a drop of Testor's liquid plastic cement. These minor details are not completely necessary since under normal circumstances they are not seen.

The .008" wire running across the entire car and through both side sills simulates the rod that operates the retainer valve, as found on the prototype. You will need to drill no. 78 holes in the side sills to accommodate this detail, which is secured to the underside of the car with a drop of cyanoacrylate adhesive (CA).

Install wire grab irons on the side and end sills by securing them with CA. Use Tichy 18" drop grab irons on the ends and Tichy 24" straight grab irons on the side sills.

Coupler box cover

Convert the coupler pocket covers so that they are held in place with 2-56 screws, which allows easy coupler installation, adjustment, and maintenance. Drill the coupler pockets and covers with no. 61 pilot holes followed by no. 50 holes to prepare them for tapping. Then tap the coupler pocket centers with a 2-56 tap. Drill the coupler pocket covers with a no. 43 clearance drill. Put the assemblies together with 2-56 fine thread machine screws

made of black engineering plastic like those sold by Kadee.

This is also a good time to install your favorite couplers and trucks. Although I prefer Kadee scale-size short-shank couplers, the medium-shank no. 158 scale size couplers work better in this situation. I used Accurail A-3 truck sideframes equipped with Reboxx semi-scale (.088"-wide tread) wheelsets. Mount the trucks with 2-56 self-tapping screws.

To act as air hose brackets, install a piece of scrap styrene to the right of each coupler pocket and inward toward the center of the car about one scale foot. When painted black, they will not show, same as with the prototype, but they will allow the 22" rubber Hi-Tech

8

Place the brass brake wheel on a wood base, hold the .015" brass staff in place, hold the soldering iron at the joint, and touch the rosin-core solder to the joint until it flows.

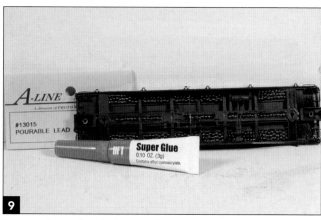

9

Super-gluing lead shot to the underside of the flatcar brings its weight up to 4 ounces, the NMRA standard.

air hoses to protrude out from under the end sills as on the prototype. A no. 70 hole is needed in each of the brackets to accept the Hi-Tech air hoses, which should be the last details installed on the model.

Vertical brake staff

The kit comes with molded styrene parts to build a vertical hand brake like on the prototype. I prefer the more durable option of an all-brass brake staff and wheel. I keep brake wheel and shaft combinations built up and at the ready for these projects by soldering the shafts to the brake wheels while the brake wheels are still on their casting sprues.

You can follow these 13 easy steps to make your own brake staffs, **8**. Purchase a package of Precision Scale brass brake wheels of your choosing and begin work while they are still on the casting sprue:

1. Open up the brake wheel centers by drilling them out with a no. 75 drill.
2. Remove the brake wheel castings from the sprue with side cuts.
3. Clean up any rough areas on the brake wheels with a fine file.
4. Lay out the brass brake wheels top down on a piece of soft scrap wood such as pine or bass wood.
5. Cut a piece of .015" straight brass rod stock 4" long for each brake wheel.
6. Using pliers, push the .015" rods through the centers of the brake

wheels and into the soft wood far enough that they stand upright independently and 90 degrees to the brake wheels.
7. Place a drop of TIX flux on each of the vertical shaft and brake wheel joints.
8. Place a small slice of TIX solder on each of the vertical shaft and brake wheel joints in the drop of flux.
9. Touch a hot 40-watt pencil soldering iron to each of the vertical shaft and brake wheel joints until the solder turns a bright silver color and flows between the two parts.
10. Allow the parts to cool and pull the parts out of the wood with a pliers.
11. Trim the shafts above the brake wheel almost even with the top of the brake wheels.
12. File the tops of the shafts flat so they look like the tops of bolt heads and file off any excess solder from the undersides of the brake wheels.
13. Trim each shaft to the required length.

Weighting the model

The completed model with trucks and couplers weighs in at about 2 ounces while the NMRA standards for a 41-foot car calls for approximately 4 ounces. The easy way to bring the car's weight up to standard is to add a permanent load, **9**. Since I wanted to

show off the real wood flooring, and I prefer removable loads for operating reasons, I rolled the car over on a block of wood to protect the vertical brake staff. I then filled every crevice of the underside with A-Line lead shot, keeping the fill levels as even as possible. When satisfied with the distribution of the lead shot, I moved the model on the block on wood to a level surface away from my work area. I then flooded the lead shot with CA and let it dry for 24 hours. The next day, I turned the car over. All the shot stayed in place, and none was visible from the side when the car was placed on the track. The wheels turned as expected and the trucks rotated as required.

Uncoupling levers

Cement a piece of .060"-square scrap styrene to the coupler pocket covers as close to the outer edges as near the center as possible. Once the solvent cement has set, drill a no. 78 hole in each of the new additions. Install Detail Associates eye bolts in the bottoms of the end sills directly below the poling pockets. Using .012" brass or phosphor bronze wire, bend uncoupling levers so that the handle ends are supported in the eye bolt's end and the coupler ends fit in the holes drilled in the styrene pieces cemented to the coupler pocket covers. A carefully placed drop of CA on the coupler ends of the cut levers will hold them in place yet allow easy removal for coupler servicing and maintenance.

Making lumber loads for a bulkhead flatcar

By Jeff Wilson

1

Bundled lumber loads can give flatcars a unique look. You can change up the size of the boards and bundles to vary the appearance among models.

Freight car loads are a great way to make a model distinctive. I added this lumber load to a Walthers model of a GSC flatcar, **1**. Although it represents a Burlington car of the mid- to late 1960s, you can do the same to almost any flatcar of that period, regardless of car style or prototype.

Through the 1950s, lumber loads were usually hand-stacked on flatcars, with vertical posts in the car's stake pockets keeping the planks aligned. When the lumber was in place, the posts were connected across the top

with boards or cables. Slack action and rough handling would sometimes shove boards way out of alignment, and loading and unloading were time consuming and labor intensive.

By the mid-1960s, the period I'm modeling, bundled lumber loads such as this one were becoming more common, **2**. Smaller bundles of planks were strapped together in bundles, allowing forklifts to lift them. They would be separated from each other and the car deck by crosswise planks, giving the forklifts access. Bundled loads were less prone to damage and easier and

By the 1960s, bundled lumber was becoming more common on flatcar loads, replacing the hand-stacked loads common before that period.

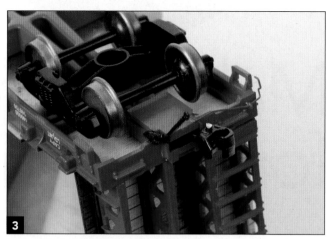

I modified the car by adding Kadee couplers and wheelsets, Cal-Scale brake hoses, and Detail Associates uncoupling levers.

Packs of sticks available in craft stores work well for making scale lumber loads.

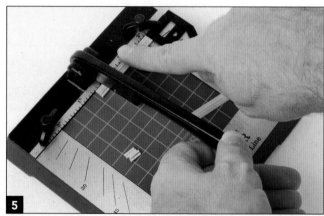

Cut the strips to length. A NorthWest Short Line Chopper is a handy tool for this.

quicker to load and unload. Beginning in the 1970s, center-beam cars began carrying more of this traffic, and covered loads became more common as well.

Prepping the car

Make any modifications to the car itself before adding the lumber load. For this car, I added an American Model Builders laser-cut wood deck (including bulkhead faces) when I first built the car several years ago. These look great, and can be glued in place or applied with peel-and-stick adhesive. I gave them a light wash of black paint to weather the surfaces.

Considering how much of the deck is covered, you can certainly keep the car's original plastic deck. I suggest painting and weathering it if you do so, starting with grimy black or flat gray and streaking (drybrushing or washes)

with various shades of dark gray, black, and brown.

I kept additional body details fairly minimal on this car. I swapped a pair of Kadee no. 5 couplers for the original couplers, but used the car's molded-in-place coupler box. I cut the steel uncoupling pin off for appearance's sake, but don't do this if you use magnetic uncouplers.

I added uncoupling levers and brake hoses on each end, **3**. Drill a no. 80 hole in the lower left corner of each end and glue a wire eye bolt in place. Thread the uncoupling lever through the eye bolt and glue the end of the lever to the edge of the coupler box lever. Glue the Cal-Scale hose bracket next to the coupler box on each end and glue the hoses in place.

I used the kit's roller-bearing truck sideframes, but I swapped Kadee smooth-back 33" wheels in place of the

kit's plastic wheels. I painted the sideframes black with streaks of roof brown and painted the wheel faces roof brown. Add the wheelsets into the frames and screw them in place on the car.

Cutting lumber

Scale lumber is available in a variety of sizes, but if you've ever decided to make a lumber load before, you've found that it takes a lot of packages of scale lumber to create even a small load, which makes it an expensive proposition. I get around this in two ways: by gluing together loads that are hollow in the middle, and by using inexpensive packages of wood strips designed for craft projects.

The wood strips I used are from a craft store, **4**. They're made by Creatology (no. 422276), but many other brands and types are available. Mine are just over 2½" long (about 18 scale feet) and .072" square.

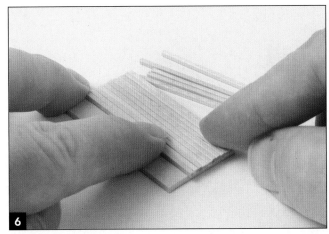

6 Use CA to glue the top layer of strips on a basswood backing sheet.

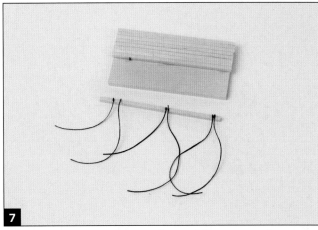

7 Glue lengths of EZ line to the middle strip in the top row to simulate straps.

8 This finished bundle has hollow ends. The EZ Line is pulled around and under the sides and glued in the inside.

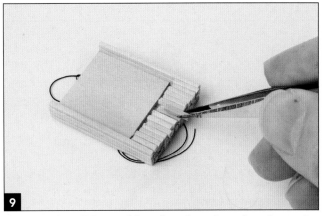

9 If the ends will be visible, glue short lengths of wood strips in place between the sides.

I decided to make my bundles a scale 16 feet long—this matches a typical prototype lumber length, and three loads of this length would just fit lengthwise between the bulkheads. I then made two additional bundles 12 scale feet long, to sit atop the bottom loads. Adjust the length to suit your car. Typical lumber lengths include 8, 10, 12, 14, and 16 feet.

Start by cutting the wood strips to length. A NorthWest Short Line Chopper (which uses a razor blade on an arm) makes short work of this task, **5**. You can set up a guide along the fence to the length you need and cut multiple strips at the same time. I test-fit the strips side by side on the car deck to determine how wide the loads needed to be. For my car, the loads had to be 17 strips wide since they had to fit between vertical posts placed in the car's stake pockets.

I found it easiest to glue the strips to a piece of basswood to keep them in alignment. Cut a piece of sheet basswood slightly shorter than the strips themselves—this will vary depending upon whether the ends of the bundles are visible. The width should be equal to the width of the load minus two strips, so 15 strips wide for my loads.

Adding the load

Begin gluing the strips to the basswood sheet with medium viscosity cyanoacrylate adhesive (CA), **6**. The CA sets much faster than white or wood glue and creates a strong bond. Be careful not to use too much, or it will ooze out of the seams.

To create the straps I used EZ Line, an elastic thread from Berkshire Junction. To simulate two side-by-side bundles, use CA to glue three or four pairs of EZ Line to one of the strips, **7**.

The line should be long enough to wrap around the load under each side. Glue this strip in place in the middle of the top layer.

Continue gluing the remaining strips across the top. Glue one strip on each edge of the top and then begin applying strips down the sides. You can glue another basswood backing piece in place to keep the strips aligned. Once the piece is the height you need, pull the EZ Line straps around the sides and glue them on the inside of the stack, **8**.

The ends of the first stacks I built would not be visible (they are hidden by each other and the car's bulkheads), so I didn't add any end pieces. For stacks that have visible ends, such as the two 12-foot-long stacks on my car, I cut the basswood backing sheet short enough to allow enough room on the ends to add short lengths of "lumber," **9**. These are just cutoffs, a few

10

When finished, the hollow bundles appear solid.

11

Glue 2 x 6 strips to the car deck and then glue the first layer of bundles in place on the 2 x 6s.

12

Use additional 2 x 6 strips to separate the first layer of bundles from the top bundles.

13

Glue 4 x 4s in the car's stake pockets to the top of the two-layer loads. Tie these posts together across the load with 2 x 6 strips.

Materials

Walthers
GSC flatcar, Chicago, Burlington & Quincy

American Model Builders/LaserKit
261, Wood deck and bulkheads for Walthers GSC flat

Berkshire Junction
EZ Line, black

Cal-Scale
190-276, Air hoses

Detail Associates
2206, Wire eye bolts
6215, Uncoupling levers

Kadee
5, Couplers
520, 33" wheelsets

Kappler scale lumber
KP1122-HOP12, Scale 2 x 6
KP1149-HOP12, Scale 4 x 4

Miscellaneous
Craft wood or scale stripwood for load

scale feet long, glued in place between the sides. They only have to be long enough to give the impression that the stack is solid, **10**.

Glue the bundles in place on the car. You can also glue the stacks to each other and make the load removable. Short pieces of scale 2 x 6 lumber rest under each bottom bundle, and between layers of bundles, **11**. I used small dabs of CA to hold everything in place, **12**.

Finish the load by adding vertical 4 x 4 posts in several of the stake pockets. These are tied together across the tops of the bundles by horizontal 2 x 6 strips, all glued in place with CA, **13**.

You can modify this technique by using strips of different dimensions and lengths and by making bundles in larger or smaller sizes.

Adding a grader load to an ITC flatcar

By Mont Switzer

1

An Illinois Terminal flatcar with a Caterpillar grader rests at the Monon/Pennsy interchange on my HO layout. The Norscot model makes a perfect load for the Proto 2000 flatcar.

Illinois Terminal Co. (ITC) was located amid various manufacturers of tractors, road-building, and other heavy equipment, including the Caterpillar Tractor Co., which built the no. 12 Diesel Motor Grader. I purchased a Norscot model of the no. 12, giving me the opportunity to load an ITC flatcar with a very visible load that could be routed over the section of the late-1950s Monon Railroad that I model, **1**.

The flatcar

I had a Proto 2000 (now Walthers) 50-ton, 53'-6" flatcar in my stash of unbuilt kits. The model is lettered for ITC 1109, one of 50 cars of this design purchased by the ITC. Likely to show up in Peoria in the late 1950s, this car was perfect for transporting the grader.

I began roughing up the car's deck molding with 80-grit sandpaper mounted to a homemade sanding block, **2**. After a thorough cleaning, I dry-brushed the deck molding with grimy black paint. Once it thoroughly dried, I lightly sanded the deck with 120-grit sandpaper to gain the effect I wanted. If you take off too much material, add

2

To improve the simulated-wood deck, paint it black and then rough up the boards with 80-grit sandpaper, while the crevices remain filled with the black paint. I also add weathering powders for effect.

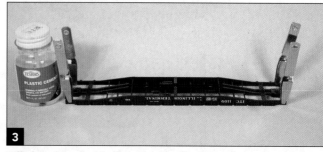

3

Fill the slots behind the side sills in each corner with black .030" styrene. Heat sink clamps hold the styrene in place for gluing. This allows for easier installation of the A-Line metal steps.

4

Note the piece of semicircular sprue material cemented to the center of the cover. This keeps the coupler end of the uncoupling lever secure. Also note the locations of the steps and grab irons.

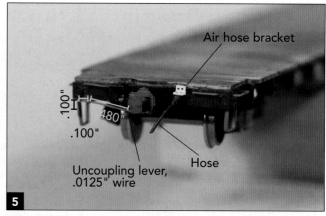

5

Air hose bracket

.100"

.480"

.100"

Uncoupling lever, .0125" wire

Hose

The air hose mounting bracket is styrene angle stock cemented to the car end sills. Four Archer Fine Transfers resin rivets give it a look of permanency when painted. The Hi Tech air hose is mounted in a hole drilled in the end sill under the bracket.

more grimy black. When satisfied with the effect, overcoat the deck with Testor's Dullcote.

I built the model as instructed with a few exceptions. The molded styrene sill steps furnished with the kit are crude by today's standards and prone to breaking. I replaced them with wire details from A-Line.

I filled the slots behind the side sills in each corner intended for the molded styrene sill steps with bits of .030"-thick black styrene, **3**. Cut these to fit the openings and hold them in place with small clamps. Touch a brush of liquid plastic cement behind each styrene bit so the cement wicks into the joint, and then set the model aside until the joint hardens.

When dry, test-fit the metal weight. Trim the newly added styrene even with the bottoms of the side sills using a single-edge razor blade and sand them even with the bottom of the side sills.

After test-fitting the major components, lay the floor top down on a flat surface and add the weight and then the body. Put a small amount of solvent cement under the coupler pockets along with the long screws that connect the weight and the floor. Add weights over the coupler pockets and allow the cement to dry overnight before handling.

Don't glue the sill bottom in place yet (its rivet detail could be damaged during installation of other details). Wait on the couplers as well, but you can test-fit the coupler-box covers at this point.

The bottoms of the coupler pocket covers are modified to hold the ends of the uncoupling levers. Add small bits of half round styrene, using leftover sprue material, **4**. Cut pieces from the sprue approximately .130" long and use liquid plastic cement to adhere them to the covers (while the covers are not installed).

Trucks and couplers

The trucks furnished with the kit have sideframes of black engineering plastic. The wheelsets have metal wheels on plastic axles with needlepoint bearings and roll very well. The problem with engineering plastic is that when unpainted it is shiny and unrealistic. You can paint the sideframes, but the material does not hold paint well. I prefer to sandblast the sideframes with a desktop (enclosed) media blasting unit.

Remove the wheelsets from the sideframes. Place pieces of masking tape over the axle bearing holes on the rear of each sideframe to protect the slick bearing surfaces and then media blast the frames (I always wear a dust mask or respirator to avoid breathing stray media dust). When the blasting is complete, remove the tape and wash the frames in soap and warm water to remove any media residue. The resulting sideframes are a realistic flat gray or

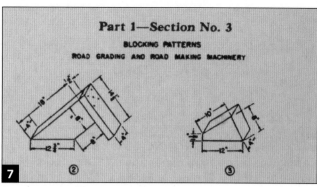

6 Cars must be reweighed on a regular basis. I simulated the repainted area here with a decal, and then added new data with another decal, which captures the cluttered look of a typical prototype restenciling job.

7 The modeled blocking follows configurations 2 and 3 on this prototype guide sheet.

grimy black color. The blasting leaves the surface porous enough for application of weathering powders.

I substituted wheelsets with metal axles and metal wheels with semi-scale (.088" wide) treads. For this model, I used ReBoxx no. WS2-1005 wheelsets. Use a small brush to paint the wheel faces, backs, and axles grimy black or dark rust brown.

I used Kadee no. 153 scale-size, short-shank whisker-spring couplers on this car. They are a drop-in fit for the car's molded coupler pockets. Weather the couplers by applying dark rust paint to the major surfaces of the couplers, but avoid getting paint in the moving parts. Also coat the glad hands on the air hoses, the brake staff, and the brake wheel. Paint the angle cocks above the air hoses the same color.

Add the wheelsets to the sideframes and install the trucks. I enhanced the sideframes by brushing on Bragdon weathering powders: dark rust on the spring packs and brake shoes to simulate rust, and brake dust and black powder around the journals to simulate oil that has leaked from the journal. You can also add gray weathering powders over the sideframes to enhance visibility.

Roll each wheelset around while scraping the paint off each tread sidewall. Track frogs, diamonds, and hump retarders tend to keep prototype sidewalls brightly polished.

Details
The kit's vertical brake staff installation is nice, but it is still a vulnerable styrene part. I prefer substituting a brass

.015" wire shaft soldered to a brass brake wheel. Glue the detail in place with cyanoacrylate adhesive (CA).

Make air hose brackets from Evergreen .060" L-angle. Slice off two pieces of the angle 8 scale inches wide to form the brackets and glue them to the end sills, immediately to the right of the coupler pocket openings and as high as possible on the end sills, **5**. Drill a no. 75 hole directly under each bracket to accommodate the Hi Tech rubber air hoses. Add the hoses, and with the angle cocks on top, stop before they are pulled under the new brackets. Trim off the excess material that protrudes from behind the end sills. Add four Archer Fine Transfers decal rivets to the tops of each bracket. They represent the two rivets that hold each bracket to the end sill and the nuts threaded onto the U-bolt that holds the hose in place.

Turn the car upside down and lay it on its deck. Drill no. 75 holes for the sill steps as shown in photo **4**, and then insert the sill steps so that they protrude a scale 12" below the bottom of their respective side sills. A drop of CA on each side sill leg will secure them. Also at this time, use liquid plastic cement to secure the kit's center sill cover.

The uncoupling levers are made from .0125" phosphor bronze wire approximately 7 scale feet long. Support the handle ends of the levers with Precision Scale eye bolts. Locate the eye bolts in the bottom of the end sills a scale 15" inboard from the side sills. First, bend handles in the cut levers so that they are .100" long, and then

follow the dimensions in photo **5**. Terminate the coupler ends of the levers in no. 78 holes drilled in the sprue pieces previously cemented to the coupler pocket covers (use a 90-degree bend in the coupler end of the levers for this). A small drop of CA secures the lever.

The side and end sills are predrilled to accommodate molded styrene grab irons. I drilled out these holes with a no. 78 bit and substituted Tichy 18" wire grabs, held with drops of CA applied from the rear.

Weathering and finishing
I wanted to keep the journal repack data fresh, so I covered that lettering with masking tape. I also wanted my car to appear to be recently reweighed, so I scraped most of the LD LMT, LT WT, and NEW location data numbers and letters off the side sills. I applied small strips of boxcar red decal paper (you can simply paint some scrap clear decal paper) where the missing numbers and letters had been, **6**. You want to leave the impression that the old numbers were painted out with whatever paint was on hand when the car was reweighed. For the missing dimensional data numbers and reweigh location lettering, I used decals from my scrapbox.

When the reweigh lettering was complete, I gave the entire car a coat of Dullcote to protect the decals and prepare it for weathering powders, which adhere well to the dull finish. Rust tends to accumulate at the bottom of the car sides so apply medium rust at that location. Add the same rust color

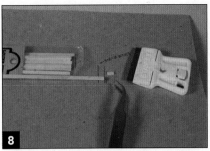

8

Cutting the wood from dimensional lumber is easier and more accurate when done on cardstock with lines drawn for cutting guides. The knife is a new single-edge razor blade in a scraper handle.

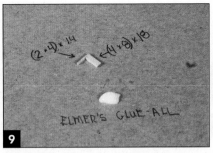

9

The blocks that go under the tires are made from two pieces of custom cut dimensional lumber assembled with Elmer's Glue-All as shown.

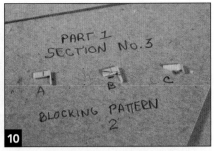

10

Draw a vertical line on the heavy piece 12" from the end. Draw a second line diagonally on the 4 x 10 piece, noting that it crosses the 2 x 4 piece that was previously glued on. Cut along the diagonal line with a sharp razor blade.

to the brake staff and brake details to enhance these areas, which also tend to show rust. Beyond that, a mild application of rust over the entire car is about all that's required before setting the car aside for a few days to allow the powders to dry and affix themselves to the model. Peel off the masking tape used to keep the journal repack data fresh.

Grader

I'm sure there are small details on the model that would jump out at someone who has worked on a prototype grader, but the one that struck me as obviously missing is window glass.

The cab is held on by a single rivet, and drilling it out frees the cab from the frame. The steering column and the right and left blade control rods, all flexible plastic details, are run into holes. Gently pull these out of the front of the cab, and it should lift off the chassis. Use tweezers to pull the interior out of the cab from the bottom. I painted the cab window frames black with a Sharpie marker, but I wonder if the time and aggravation was worth the minimal improvement in the model's appearance. You be the judge on your model.

I cut four cab window panels from Evergreen .005" clear styrene. Each panel covers all the window openings on that side. Secure each panel in the cab with a drop of Micro Kristal Klear. It dries clear and glossy so that any exposed cement is not noticeable.

Prepare the cab for reassembly by drilling out the hole in the cab tab and

grader frame with a no. 50 bit. Tap both holes with a 2-56 tap, fit both parts together, and join them with a ⅛"-long, 2-56 screw. Test-fit the screw from the bottom. It should hold both parts together, yet not be visible when the model is viewed from the side.

Paint the operator's seat cushion and seat back black and then fit the interior back inside the cab. Fit the cab to the frame and then add the screw from the bottom, adjusting the cab so that it sets level. Insert the steering column and the two blade control rods back into their respective holes.

Blocking

Wood blocking is used on prototype cars to secure equipment to the deck. Specific rules govern how actual blocking is constructed for prototype railroads, how it is secured to the car deck, and how it secures various pieces of road-making equipment. We'll use two types (configurations 2 and 3) patterned after the prototype diagram, **7**.

I made my blocks from Kappler HO scale dimensional lumber. You'll need four different lengths of wood:

3	1 x 6 x scale 24" (for placement under grader blade)
8	2 x 4 x scale 14" (for cementing to end of 4 x 10 x scale 18")
8	4 x 8 x scale 18" (for cementing to 2 x 4 x scale 14")
6	4 x 10 x scale 12" (for cutting to side chocks in configuration 3)

I made all of the cuts with a new single-edge razor blade mounted in a plastic blade holder for easier and safer

use and glued pieces together (and to the deck) with Elmer's Glue-All. As photo **8** shows, I marked the needed dimensions on a piece of cardboard and cut all the strips to length.

Before placing the grader on the flatcar deck, turn it over. Apply three small dots of Elmer's Glue-All to the bottom of the grader blade and place the three 1 x 6 boards in the spots. Straighten them and let them dry.

If you were to drive the grader onto the flatcar deck, once you had it properly positioned in the center, you would set the brakes. In HO scale, you do this by placing a drop of CA on one side of one drive axle so it won't roll while you install the blocking. Glue the six chocks cut from pattern 3, three per side against the outside of the tires, to secure the grader against sideways movement.

Glue the remaining eight chocks together from the previously cut 2 x 4s and 4 x 10s, and trimmed to the proper shape, **9** and **10**. Glue four of these chocks in the front and rear of the steering tires, two in front of the front drive tires, and two behind the rear drive tires.

All this blocking will not hold if the car is switched over a hump or subjected to other forms of rough handling. DO NOT HUMP signs are required on all sides of the car to warn crews. Jaeger makes these placards. Glue four of them to thin cardstock, cut them out, and glue them to 2 x 4 basswood posts. Install them in a stake pocket on each side and on each end of the car, as seen in photo **1**. Your grader is now ready to be shipped to a dealer.

Modernizing a Sioux City wood reefer

By Jeff Wilson

1

Several years ago, 5th Avenue Car Shops produced a special run of Accurail wood refrigerator cars lettered for National Car Co. (reporting marks NX) with a Sioux City Dressed Beef logo. NCC was a subsidiary of the Fruit Growers Express, set up to provide cars to various packing companies. A good part of the NCC fleet included older wood cars that had been rebuilt and repainted. This model represents such a car that was rebuilt in the late 1950s.

A photo of a similar car appeared in the book *Refrigerator Car Color Guide* by Gene Green (Morning Sun, 2005). I decided to upgrade the model to match the prototype by adding underframe details, adding a power brake, adding separate ladders and grab irons, and touching up the paint, **1**. You can follow these techniques in modernizing many other upgraded wood refrigerator cars.

Modeling
The Accurail car has separate sides that press into place on the body shell, so start by removing the sides from the shell and removing the injection-molded (simulated wood) running board.

Many older wood-side refrigerator cars were rebuilt in the 1940s and '50s, which extended their service lives into the 1960s. That was the case for the prototype of this Accurail HO kit, custom decorated by 5th Avenue Car Shops in a late 1950s Sioux City Dressed Beef scheme.

2 Carefully remove the molded-on ladder detail with a chisel-tip hobby knife. Work slowly—don't try to remove all the material in one pass—and keep the blade at a low angle to the surface.

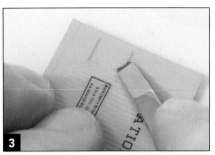

3 A Micro-Mark detail-removal chisel also works well for cutting off molded-on parts. Its design makes it less likely to gouge the surface than a knife blade.

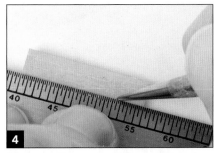

4 Use a scriber to continue the car's vertical board grooves through the areas where the molded-on details were located. A straightedge guides the scriber.

5 Cut down the new ladders to size and airbrush them yellow before gluing them in place on the car sides.

6 A new ladder and grab irons have been applied to the end. I painted the exposed part of the side yellow to match the prototype.

7 The end ladder, grab irons, and brake gear have been applied to the B end of the shell.

I decided to remove the molded-on side ladders, end ladders, and grab irons and replace them with separate pieces. This is, of course, optional—you may find the updated appearance worth it, or decide that the effort is too tedious and simply isn't worth the time.

Start by using a chisel-tip knife blade or Micro-Mark detail chisel to shave off the molded-on details, **2** and **3**. The key is to keep the blade flat to the surface to avoid gouging it, and to work slowly, not trying to shave off too much at once. The detail chisel is more expensive, but I find it offers much more control compared to a blade. Touch up any areas as needed with fine sandpaper.

You'll need to touch up areas where these details crossed the vertical grooves of the car siding. I used a scriber to add grooves in these areas, following the guide of a steel rule as a straightedge, **4**. Work slowly and try to match the existing grooves as closely as possible.

Touch up the modified areas as needed. I used a brush, although an airbrush would be ideal. Paint matching is an inexact science. I tried various shades of yellow for the sides, and wound up using Modelflex reefer yellow for the sides and a mix of light Tuscan oxide red and dark Tuscan oxide red for the ends. The colors aren't exact matches, but—with some weathering—they ended up being close enough. I also brush-painted the bottom of the sides on the shell yellow to match the prototype car, as the model had these exposed strips in red.

For the new ladders, I looked through my scrapbox and found some ladders from an old boxcar kit and cut them down to a six-rung height, **5**. I airbrushed them the same yellow and

Materials

5th Avenue Car Shops
Accurail refrigerator car,
   Sioux City Dressed Beef

American Model Builders
293, 40-foot wood running board

Cal-Scale
190-276, Brake hoses
190-283, AB brake gear set

Detail Associates
2206, Wire eye bolts
6215, Uncoupling levers
6242, Ladders

InterMountain
40050, 33" scale wheelsets

Kadee
2020, Ajax brake wheel

Tichy
3021, 18" scale grab irons

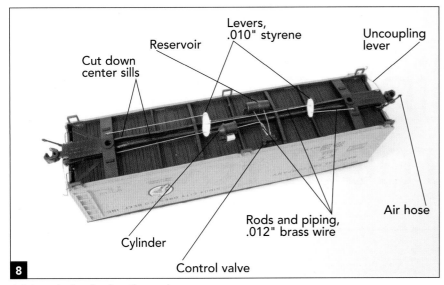

Cut down center sills
Reservoir
Levers, .010" styrene
Uncoupling lever
Cylinder
Rods and piping, .012" brass wire
Control valve
Air hose

8

Add underbody details as shown.

9

The sides received a light wash of black and rust-color oil paint, streaked down the side to match the boards.

red that I had used on the body. Detail Associates no. 6242 ladders will also work, but they'll need to be cut down as well. I added a few small dots of cyanoacrylate adhesive (CA) along the back of the vertical posts and carefully set each ladder in place on the car.

For the new wire grab irons, drill mounting holes using the marks from the old molded-on irons as reference. Add a bit of CA to the ends of the grabs and insert them in the mounting holes. You'll have to drill clearance holes in the body shell behind the side grabs as shown in photo **6**.

The kit includes the older style vertical brake staff with the brake wheel mounted horizontally atop the staff. When these cars were rebuilt, most received new brake wheels mounted on the car ends. Glue the new brake wheel housing and platform on the B end,

along with the Kadee brake wheel and paint them to match the end, **7**.

The model had the deep fish-belly center sills of USRA-style cars, but the prototype had a straight center sill. I simply cut down the kit's center sill, **8**. The other brake components are glued in place, with brass wire rods and piping as shown in photo **8**. I also added Cal-Scale air hoses and Detail Associates uncoupling levers at each end.

The trucks are the kit's original frames, but I substituted InterMountain scale 33" metal wheelsets. I painted the wheel faces rail brown, and then added Testor's CreateFX oil and grease to simulate the effects of journal box oil leaking onto the wheels.

Weathering
I weathered the car using artist's oil colors, placing small dabs of black,

brown, and rust colors in an aluminum palette. Then I touched a turpentine-filled brush to a color and streaked it on the car. I used black on the roof with various browns on the sides, **9**. You can make this effect as light or heavy as you like, depending on how old you want your car to appear.

I removed the kit's injection-molded running board before working on the car, and decided to replace it with a laser-cut wood part from American Model Builders. Before installing the running board, I painted it with washes of boxcar red, letting some wood grain show through. I added a bit of super glue to each running board support on the roof, and then carefully set the piece in place, **10** and **11**. The car is now ready for service.

10

Add a bit of super glue to the running board supports along the center of the roof.

11

Press the new wood running board in place, making sure it's aligned properly.

Upgrading a Wilson meat reefer

By Jeff Wilson

1

A few detail upgrades along with some weathering brought this Walthers model closer to the Wilson meat reefer that it is designed to represent.

Packing companies operated large fleets of ice-bunker refrigerator cars through the 1960s. Among the larger operators was Wilson & Co., and this project looks at adding details to a kit to get its appearance closer to its intended prototype, **1**.

The model represents one of 800 steel refrigerator cars Wilson purchased in 1957 (nos. 2000–2799), **2**. They followed the same construction as other meat reefers of the period. They were 42 feet long with a horizontal overlapping seam down the middle of each side.

Walthers first came out with a kit for this car in the 1990s, **3**. I built several of them at the time, and Walthers recently reissued this car as a ready-to-run model, and you can apply many of these techniques to that model as well.

There are a few differences between the prototype and model. The prototype has a straight side sill, while the model has slight steps at each end (Walthers has offered two versions of this body, neither with a straight sill). The model shows an air-circulating fan, which the prototype lacks. The tack board location also doesn't match. The doors on

2 Wilson purchased 800 42-foot steel refrigerator cars in 1957. Many ran until the end of the ice-bunker reefer era (300 were in service in 1973). *Jeff Wilson collection*

3 The model, as built straight from the box, differs from the prototype in a few areas.

4 Use a straightedge to guide the knife blade when cutting off the drop-down tab along each side.

5 Carefully shave the crossbearers so that the bottom of each end is even with the bottom of the car side.

the prototype were 6'-4" tall, but on the model they are taller (going to the roof). Finally, the ends aren't an exact match. I upgraded as many of these items as I could while keeping the model's paint scheme intact. I decided modifying the doors and ends would be too involved.

Sill and underbody

Start by trimming the lower, long tab from each side to create a straight

edge, **4**. Hold a ruler along the side and make several light passes with a hobby knife until the piece is cut completely through. Clean up the edge with a needle file or sanding stick if necessary.

This exposes the lower part of the ends on a few of the underframe cross members. Trim these by shaving down the thickness of the cross members with a chisel-tip knife blade, again making light passes to remove material, **5**.

The model's brake gear is not in the right location, and the detail is lacking. Trim it all away and discard it, and then replace the parts with a Cal-Scale brake set and .012" wire to represent pipes and rods. Photo **6** shows the location for all the components, which I estimated based on several prototype photos. (For details on installing them, see project 3, pages 12–14, and project 22, page 91.)

The corner steps on the model are not the correct style, so I replaced them, as well as the steps beneath each side door, with A-Line's much sturdier wire steps. I added small strips of styrene behind the sides at the step locations to provide more room for drilling mounting holes for the steps.

Finish the underbody details with uncoupling levers and brake hoses at each end. I also added Kadee no. 5 couplers in the model's coupler boxes.

Body

I decided to change the location of the tack board to match the prototype. To do this, remove the molded-on tack

Stirrup steps

Reservoir

Levers, .010" styrene

Styrene shims

Cylinder

Mounting pads, .060" styrene

Control valve

Rods and piping, .012" wire

6 Add the new Cal-Scale brake components, .012" wire piping and levers, and wire steps to the underframe.

7

Cut away the molded tack board with a chisel-tip hobby knife blade. Work slowly and make multiple passes.

8

Sand the area smooth. Squadron's flexible sanding pads work well for this. Use tape to protect the surrounding area.

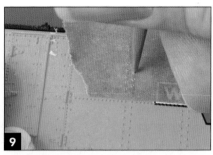

9

Use tape and a scriber to transfer the rivet pattern from an adjoining rivet line to the sanded area.

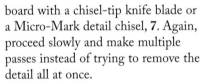

10

Embossing the rivet areas with a scriber creates a shadow effect.

11

Use a wide, soft brush to paint the sanded area with a matching color. It may take two or three coats to cover completely.

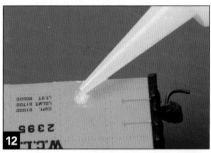

12

CA works well as a body filler. Add a drop of accelerator after applying the CA.

board with a chisel-tip knife blade or a Micro-Mark detail chisel, **7**. Again, proceed slowly and make multiple passes instead of trying to remove the detail all at once.

Smooth the area with a fine sanding stick (my favorites are Squadron's flexible sticks), starting with medium grit and then proceeding to fine and extra fine, **8**. Masking the area around the area being sanded helps protect the surface, rivets, and other details. Continue sanding until the area is smooth.

The blank area is lacking rivet detail. You can treat this in a couple of ways. I pressed a piece of masking tape over a neighboring vertical rivet line, marked the rivets with a pencil, and placed the tape over the blank area. I poked a scriber at the pencil locations to mark the surface, **9**. Pressing the scriber harder into the surface leaves indentations roughly the same size as surrounding raised rivets, **10**, and after weathering, the difference isn't readily apparent, especially from normal viewing distance.

If I were doing this again, I would use Archer Fine Transfers rivet heads

(no. AR88025), a product that I didn't discover until after this project was complete. The small rounded resin details, representing rivets, come on clear decal film. You apply the rivets like regular decals.

Paint the area, matching the model's original paint as closely as possible, **11**. This is a hit-and-miss process. There's no magic way to match paint, as each model manufacturer uses different paint—none of which matches available model paints. I found that Polly Scale Daylight orange was pretty close to the original Walthers car. Either mask the area and airbrush it, or do as I did and use a wide, soft brush. Use brush strokes from top to bottom, in the same way later weathering will be applied. It will take two or three coats to cover the area thoroughly.

I also removed the fan connector detail (the small circular molding at the lower left on each side). Meat reefers such as this one rarely had air-circulating fans. I used a chisel to remove the raised detail, but since the middle of the circle was depressed, it needed to be filled. Instead of mod-

eling putty, I prefer medium viscosity cyanoacrylate adhesive (CA) for this, as CA cures instantly with accelerator, dries hard, and can be shaped and sanded.

Apply a drop of CA to fill the indentation, **12**. Next, apply a drop of CA accelerator (such as Insta-Set or Insta-Cure) to the CA with a pipette or eyedropper. (Don't use the sprayer on the accelerator bottle, as it will make a mess over a large area, and the accelerator can damage some types of paint.) The CA will cure instantly so be sure to wipe off any excess accelerator.

Use a knife or chisel to shape the area as with the tack board, **13**. Then sand the area smooth and paint it.

My tack boards are from my scrapbox, but Sylvan Scale Models, ProtoLoads, and others offer them as separate items. Paint the new tack boards orange and glue them in place with CA. The large one goes low on the side just to the right of the reporting marks; the small (route) board goes below that, just above the bottom edge of the side.

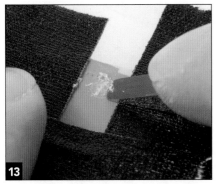

13 Shape the hardened CA with a chisel and sanding stick after it has cured.

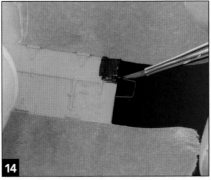

14 Paint the area below the door black on each side.

15 Weather the roof by scraping gray chalk with a knife and then brushing the powder in place with a stiff brush.

16 Paint the steel running board black. If using a brush, dab the paint on instead of using brush strokes.

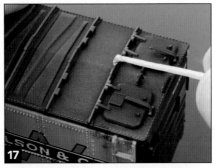

17 Use a toothpick to apply E-6000 adhesive to each running board support and then set the running board in place.

18 The new running board has a slim profile that's much more realistic than the original injection-molded item.

The prototype cars are painted black under each door. Mask the ends of this area, and then carefully paint the area black with a fine brush, **14**.

I decided to replace the model's heavy cast-plastic running board with an etched-metal part from Plano. I began by weathering the black roof, brushing it with several shades of medium and dark gray chalk, **15**. I then sealed it with a light overspray of clear flat finish.

Paint the running board black. An airbrush or spray can works well. If you use a brush, dabbing the paint in place works better than using regular brush strokes (a couple of coats will be needed), **16**.

My favorite adhesive for affixing metal running boards is E-6000, a strong, clear, flexible permanent cement, **17**. It stays flexible (unlike CA), so it works well for joining dissimilar materials like plastic and metal. Use a toothpick to apply a coat of E-6000 on each of the running board supports, and then set the running board in place, **18**.

Final paint and weathering

Paint the underframe and truck sideframes black. (I use a 1:1 mix of black and grimy black.) I substituted Kadee smooth-back scale 33" metal wheels for the original kit wheels. Paint the wheel faces, backs, and axles roof brown. Weather the truck sideframes and couplers with streaks of dark rust colors and the wheel faces with black (to represent journal-box grease).

I used oil paint washes for weathering on the sides (see page 91 for more details), with raw sienna for light rust colors and burnt sienna and burnt umber for dark rust colors. I concentrated heavier streaks running downward from the ice hatches in each corner—the salt that was often added to the brine tanks typically caused more corrosion and staining in these areas. I finished weathering by brushing and then drybrushing a few light white streaks in the same areas. To finish, seal all of the weathering with a light coat of clear flat finish.

Materials

Walthers
Wilson meat refrigerator car

A-Line
29000, Stirrup steps

Cal-Scale
190-276, Brake hoses
190-283, Brake set

Detail Associates
2206, Wire eye bolts
2504, Wire, .012" brass
6215, Uncoupling lever

Kadee
5, Couplers
520, Wheelsets

Plano
191, Metal running board, slotted

Modeling GN ore cars in gravel service

By Cody Grivno

1

This former Great Northern ore car is spending its last years in gravel service on the Burlington Northern.

With a six-pack of GN ore cars at the ready, I set out to model some ore cars reassigned to gravel service, **1**. If there is one person to thank for this project, it's my father, Steve. While I was combing through his negative collection, I came across images of Great Northern ore cars, **2**. My interest was piqued because the shots were taken in the yard in Crookston, Minn., my hometown.

Crookston is on the opposite side of Minnesota from the Iron Range, but it wasn't uncommon for ore cars to migrate across the state after the shipping season closed on Lake Superior. In the late fall and winter, the cars were used to transport sugar beets from piling stations in outlying areas to processing plants in Crookston and Moorhead. But these cars didn't have BEET LOADING ONLY stencils. Instead, they had stencils that read SUPERIOR WIS GRAVEL SERV ONLY.

Prepping the cars

The first step in the project was to disassemble the Wm. K. Walthers 24-foot Minnesota ore cars and wash them in warm water and dish soap. This removes skin oils and other impurities that might affect paint adhesion. I then let the models air dry on a lint-free towel. For the duration of the project, I only handled the models while wearing latex gloves.

Next, for each model, I weathered the plastic body and die-cast metal underframe using thinned Model Master engine black, grimy black, and oxide red (9 parts paint to 1 part 70 percent isopropyl alcohol). I built up the weathering in light layers, using prototype photos as a guide.

After the weathering colors had dried, I used an airbrush to spray the model with Model Master gloss clear, **3**. This provides a smooth, glossy surface for the decals.

From iron ore to gravel

Not surprisingly, there are no commercial decals for SUPERIOR WIS GRAVEL SERV ONLY stencils, so I had to make my own. A quick Internet search for a stencil font turned up Boston Traffic, a decent match to the lettering on the full-size car. Better yet, the font was a free download. The smallest decal sheet I could get from Circus City Decals & Graphics was 5½" x 8½", so I added some other Burlington Northern-related lettering to help fill out the sheet.

It took less than a week to get the decals. Per the manufacturer's recommendation, I applied a coat of Microscale Liquid Decal Film to the sheet to protect the ink. After 15 minutes, the decals were ready to use.

I first applied the SUPERIOR WIS GRAVEL SERV ONLY and D-76 lettering from the custom-produced decal set. Then I applied Microscale black trim film over data printed on the model. I used repack data from Champion Decal Co. set HB-389 to indicate that the solid-bearing journals had been serviced, **4**. I applied Micro Sol to the decals to help them conform to irregular surfaces on the model. Any stubborn decals received a light application of the more aggressive Solvaset.

With all the decals in place, I gently wiped the model with a cloth and

This full-size car inspired this project. *Steve Grivno, Cody Grivno collection*

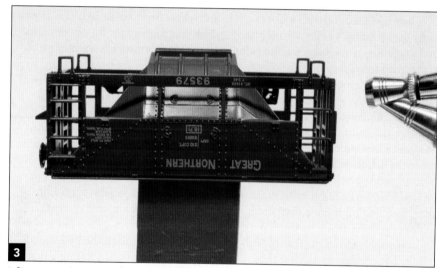

I first weathered the ore car with thinned Model Master engine black, grimy black, and oxide red. Then I applied a gloss clear coat to prepare the model for decaling.

distilled water. The water removes glue and other impurities from the decaling process. I prefer distilled water for this as it's less likely to leave mineral deposits, which may dry as little white spots on the model.

Then I sprayed the sides of the car with a thin coat of Model Master gloss clear. This seals the decals and prevents future weathering from potentially wicking behind the decals.

Interior weathering

This car is designed to run empty or loaded, so I weathered the interior. I cut a mask from a manila file folder and sprayed the interior with Model Master grimy black, earth, and leather, using an overhead shot of an ore car as a guide, **5**.

I let the paint dry thoroughly (until there was no discernible odor) before spraying the body and underframe with Model Master flat clear. This gave the car a realistic flat finish and made the edges of the decals hard to detect.

Trucks and wheels

The truck sideframes on the Walthers model were black, but on the full-size cars they were oxide red. To remedy this, I first replaced the metal wheelsets with plastic ones. The plastic wheelsets

4

I used a combination of custom and commercial decals to enhance the realism of the ore cars. The contrasting color beneath the repack stencil was common on cars with solid-bearing trucks.

protect the sockets from paint and other residue that might prevent the metal wheels from rolling freely.

Then I painted the trucks Corsa Gray using Tamiya's spray for polycarbonate. As the name suggests, the paint is designed to stick to polycarbonate and slippery engineering plastic found on many of today's models. Better yet, the paint can be covered with acrylics.

Once the paint dried, I airbrushed the sideframes with Model Master oxide red. I followed that with a thin coat of engine black on and near the journal boxes. The black paint suggests the grease and oil residue that often built up in these areas.

I then sprayed the sideframes with Model Master flat clear. After that dried, I carefully airbrushed the journal boxes with that company's semi-gloss clear, which gives the black paint a slight sheen, further reinforcing the look of oil and grease, **6**.

I replaced the stock wheels with InterMountain 33" metal wheelsets.

After cleaning the wheels with a cotton swab and 70 percent isopropyl alcohol, I used a Microbrush to paint the axle and wheel backs oxide red. The dried color was too vibrant for my taste, so I toned it down with a wash of grimy black.

The wheel faces on the prototype cars had a caked-on layer of oil and grease. To replicate that look in HO scale, I painted the wheel faces grimy black, being careful to keep the color off the needlepoint axles. After the paint dried, I poured a small amount of Acrylicos Vallejo satin varnish in a 3-ounce plastic cup and dumped in some AIM Products grimy black weathering powder. I mixed the two ingredients with a craft stick, creating a paste that I applied with a Microbrush, **7**.

Making a mold

The ore cars don't include loads, so I had to make my own. I made patterns from ¾" extruded-foam insulation board (using David Popp's article from the April 2012 issue of *Model Railroader* as a guide).

Since the shape and height of the gravel loads vary from car to car, I made a base pattern that fit into the car and three patterns that attached to the top with different profiles. I cut the foam with a utility knife (make sure it has a sharp blade or you'll tear the foam) and shaped it with sanding sponges, **8**.

With the patterns complete, I built a mold box using plate glass and wood paint sticks. First, I attached the foam patterns to the glass floor using DAP Dynaflex 230 sealant, keeping a ½" between each one. Do not use solvent-based sealants or adhesives, as they will dissolve the foam.

I then built the walls using wood paint stir sticks. I positioned the sticks so there was at least ½" of clearance on all sides of the patterns. Once I was satisfied with the positioning of the sticks, I secured them to the glass with hot glue. To prevent the mold-making material from leaking out of the box, I liberally sealed the seams of the wall panels and where the sticks met the glass with more hot glue, **9**.

I used Alumilite's Super Casting Kit to make the silicone rubber mold, **10**. The two-part material consists of a catalyst and base, mixed at a ratio of 2:1. My mold required 16 ounces of base and 8 scoops of catalyst. I stirred the two ingredients thoroughly, scraping the sides and bottom of the mixing cup and making sure there were no swirls. Don't stir the material too vigorously, or you'll create air bubbles. The material has a 30-minute working time, so you don't need to rush. Wear latex

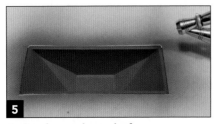

5

A simple mask made from a manila file folder was all I needed to protect the car sides when weathering the interior. I used prototype photos as a guide when weathering the models.

6

Prototype photos indicated that many Great Northern ore cars had oxide red trucks. I primed the plastic sideframes with a hobby paint designed for polycarbonates before applying Model Master oxide red.

7

The wheel faces on cars with solid-bearing trucks were often caked with a layer of oil and grease. I simulated that with Acrylicos Vallejo satin varnish and AIM Products grimy black weathering powders.

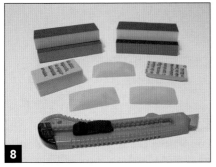

8 I made patterns for the gravel loads using ¾" extruded-foam insulation board.

9 A piece of plate glass and wood paint sticks make an easy mold box. I sealed the seams in the box and the edges where the sticks meet the glass with hot glue.

10 Alumilite's Super Casting Kit contains all you need for making molds and pouring castings. You can find it at well-stocked hobby shops and arts and crafts stores.

11 After letting the silicone rubber cure for 18 hours, I carefully removed one wall from the mold box and then gently lifted the mold from the box.

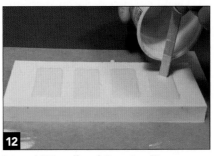

12 I used Woodland Scenics Super Strength Plaster to pour the castings. Make sure the mold is on a level surface, and work on a piece of cardboard to catch any spills.

13 I set a piece of plate glass on top of the mold to ensure mating faces of the castings would be flat. If you skip this step, you'll have a lot of sanding to do.

14 The castings can be carefully removed from the mold after about 30 minutes. If you get air bubbles in the castings, fill them with plaster or spackle and sand the patch smooth.

15 Sanding sponges make it easy to clean up rough edges on the castings. Check your work often, as it easier to remove more material than try to add more.

16 I used wood glue to attach the top half of the casting to the bottom. Wipe any glue that oozes out with a damp paper towel.

gloves and work in a well-ventilated area while mixing and pouring the mold-making rubber.

Since I was pouring the silicone over a non-silicone surface, the instructions indicated mold release wasn't required. I slowly poured the silicone in one corner of the box and let it flow over the patterns. Do not pour the mold-making rubber directly on the patterns.

The silicone has a drying time of 8 to 18 hours. I erred on the side of caution and let it dry for the full 18 hours. Then I gently removed one end of the box and carefully lifted out the mold, **11**.

Pouring castings
When the mold was completed, it was time to make the castings. I used

Woodland Scenics Super Strength Plaster, although resin would also work. Following the instructions, I added 2½ ounces of plaster to 1 ounce of water. After letting the ingredients rest for two minutes, I used a craft stick to mix the plaster with the water.

With the mold on a flat surface, I slowly poured in the plaster, using the

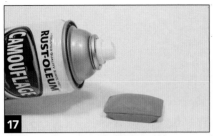

17 After sealing the plaster with Testor's Dullcote, I spray-painted the castings with Rust-Oleum khaki. The color, part of the Camouflage line, dries to a flat finish.

18 Instead of watching the paint dry, I worked on the load material. Here, I'm sifting Quikrete Tubesand through a pair of pantyhose.

19 I applied a 50:50 mixture of white glue and water to the castings. With the glue still wet, I sprinkled in the sand. The box below caught the runoff.

stirring stick as a guide, **12**. Once the mold was filled, I put a piece of plate glass on top of the mold and weighed it down with a brick to ensure that the castings would be flat, **13**. Some plaster may ooze out of the mold, so it's best to work on a piece of cardboard.

Fine tuning

I let the plaster set for about 30 minutes before carefully pulling the castings from the mold, **14**. At this point, the castings are still green (soft), so I set them on another piece of plate glass to dry. The glass has a flat surface, so the yet-to-cure castings won't warp.

No matter how good the mold is, some touch-up work is necessary on the castings. I used a fine/extra fine sanding sponge to clean up the castings' edges, **15**. Then I used wood glue to attach the top casting to the base, **16**.

Once the glue had dried, I sprayed the assembled castings with Testor's Dullcote. Plaster is very porous and soaks up paint like a sponge. This step made it easier for the final color, Rust-Oleum khaki, to cover in two coats, **17**.

While I was waiting for the paint to dry, I sifted Quikrete Tubesand to use for the load. First, I ran it through a fine kitchen-style sifter. The granules still looked too big (the pieces were about the size of an HO scale figure's hand), so I sifted the sand again using pantyhose stretched over a small plastic container, **18**. This may have been as tedious as it sounds, but it beat watching paint dry.

Finally, I coated the top of sand each load with a 50:50 mixture of white glue and water. While the glue was still wet, I sprinkled on the sand, working over a box that would collect any runoff, **19**. Using a pipette, I then soaked the sand with 70 percent isopropyl alcohol and set the loads aside to dry.

Ready for service

The last step was to reassemble the ore cars, add the trucks and couplers, and then set the loads in place. A cut of these cars behind a high-hood Electro-Motive Division GP9 would certainly look at home on a late 1970s or early 1980s Burlington Northern branch line layout set in Minnesota. Hey, that gives me an idea…

Materials

Acrylicos Vallejo
70.522, Satin varnish

AIM Products
110-3102, Grimy Black weathering
 powder

Alumilite
Super casting kit

Champion Decal
HB-389, Burlington Northern boxcar
 (for repack data)

Circus City Decals & Graphics
(circusdecals.com)
"Superior Gravel Service Only"
 custom decals

DAP Products
Dynaflex 230 clear sealant

Microscale
TF-2, Black trim film

Quikrete
1159-75, Tubesand

Rust-Oleum
1917, Camouflage Khaki

Tamiya for Polycarbonates
PS-32, Corsa Gray

Testor acrylic paint
4636, Flat Clear
4637, Semi-Gloss Clear

4638, Gloss Clear
4674, Leather
4877, Earth
4882, Oxide Red
4887, Grimy Black
4888, Engine Black

Wm. K. Walthers
910-58005, GN Minnesota ore cars

Woodland Scenics
C1199, Super strength plaster

Miscellaneous
Acrylic sealant
Hot glue
Plate glass
Sanding sponges (various grits)

Placing sheep and cattle in stock cars

By Jeff Wilson

1

Improvements to this factory-painted Accurail car include distressed side boards, bedding protruding from the sides, a load of steers, and details on the ends and underbody.

Railroads carried a lot of livestock traffic from the steam era into the 1960s, when trucks and changing markets eroded the rail business. Weathering your stock cars and adding animal loads will help you more realistically model this traffic.

You can follow these techniques with almost any stock car model, but be aware that it's best to start with a kit so you have easy access to the interior—most factory-assembled models are already glued together, making access difficult. I modified a pair of cars: an Accurail kit lettered for Illinois Central,

1, and a Proto 2000 Mather stock car decorated for Chicago, Burlington & Quincy, **2**.

Interior and underbody

Prototype stock cars were either single deck or double deck, **3**. Single-deck cars carried cattle, while double-deck cars carried smaller animals, mainly sheep and pigs. Some cars were convertible, with an upper deck that could be retracted or removed. I decided to give the single-deck IC car a load of steers, and I added a load of sheep to the double-deck Burlington car.

2 This double-deck Proto 2000 Mather stock car received a load of sheep as well as light overall weathering.

3 The sheep aboard this Burlington double-deck stock car are readily visible in this 1960s view. *Collection of Jay Williams/Big Four Graphics*

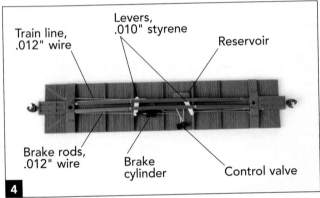

Train line, .012" wire
Levers, .010" styrene
Reservoir
Brake rods, .012" wire
Brake cylinder
Control valve

4 Underbody gear includes basic piping and rods along with levers and brake hardware.

5 The new floor is Northeastern scribed basswood, glued in place with super glue and weathered with a grimy black wash.

6 Arrange the cattle so they are close to the car sides. The goal is to provide shadows and shapes that you can see from the side when looking through the car.

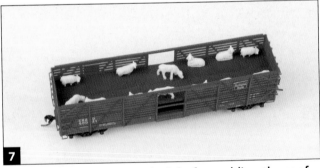

7 Add sheep to the upper deck before adding the roof. Check height clearance before gluing the sheep in place.

The Proto car had a detailed underbody, but I added several details to the Accurail underbody, **4**. Additions included a Cal-Scale brake set, along with a train line, other brake piping, levers, and rods. (See project 3, pages 12–14, for more detail on adding these optional details.)

The Accurail car had a plain plastic floor, with a large sheet metal weight designed to simply be glued or taped

to it. I added a new floor of scribed basswood (I used Northeastern 1⁄16" sheet with 1⁄16" spacing), secured to the kit's floor with super glue and trimmed to clear the body. I stained the floor with an acrylic stain of black and brown paint (mixed with about 8 parts water), **5**. This was a bit of overkill, since the floor can't really be seen through the side slats, but I wanted to be sure.

The steers don't have to be well detailed, as you'll only see the shadows and shapes of them through the sides. I had a set of Model Power cows ready, but then I found a set of 100 unpainted HO steers on eBay. I painted some with brown craft paint and super-glued them in position around the floor, **6**. Keep them as close to the car sides as possible.

On the Proto 2000 car, I started by painting the floor and the second-deck

8

Drybrush random boards with gray, and then streak gray and grimy black downward along the bottom of each side.

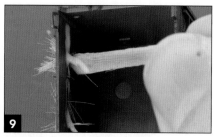

9

Add matte medium from the interior into the side gaps, and then push the field grass in place from the outside.

10

Once the matte medium dries, trim the field grass with scissors.

pieces grimy black. I prepped a package of Atlas sheep by cutting them from their thick plastic bases. The sheep can then be glued in place with super glue, again keeping them close to the sides for best visibility.

Add the two halves of the second deck and glue them in place. Glue the sheep to the floor along the sides as on the main floor. I ran out of sheep, so I added a few unpainted white calves from the set of steers—I figured once the car was sealed, nobody would be able to tell the difference, **7**. Glue the roof in place and finish assembling the kit.

Weathering

The wood slats on stock cars are often heavily weathered. The IC car was meant to be older, so I weathered it more extensively. Start by distressing several individual boards with a razor saw, knife, and sanding stick (described in project 10 on page 41). You can do this to any extent you wish, depending upon the desired age of the car.

I used a mix of washes of grimy black and gray paint on some individual boards and followed this with drybrushing, **8**. Then I gave the entire body a wash of thinned black paint (1 part engine black to 10 parts thinner).

Since the Burlington model represented a car that, although older, had been repainted only a few years previously, I gave it a lighter weathering treatment. I added gray drybrushing on several boards but no overall black wash.

I painted the trucks on both cars a mix of grimy black, black, and roof brown. I used roof brown on the wheel faces followed by washes of black.

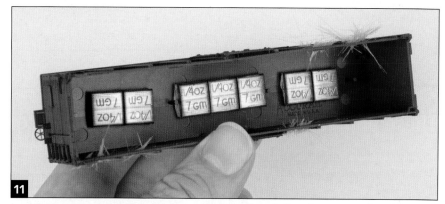

11

I added peel-and-stick weights to the roof to keep them out of sight.

Materials

Accurail
Stock car kit

Walthers
Proto 2000 Mather stock car kit

Atlas
779, Sheep

Cal-Scale
190-276, Brake hoses
190-283, Brake set

Detail Associates
2206, Wire eye bolts
2504, Wire, .012" brass
6215, Uncoupling levers

Kadee
5, Couplers
520, 33" wheelsets

Model Power
5742, Cows

Northeastern
Scribed wood sheet,
    1⁄16" thick, 1⁄16" spacing

On many prototype stock cars, you could see straw bedding being pushed out of the slat openings just above the floor. I replicated this feature using Woodland Scenics harvest gold field grass. I added acrylic matte medium to a gap and then trimmed a pinch off and shoved it into the glue from outside the car, **9**. I used matte medium because it dries with a flat finish and is virtually invisible once it dries. When the matte medium dried, I trimmed the grass with a small scissors, **10**.

I placed A-Line peel-and-stick lead weights to the inside roof of the Accurail car to make up for the missing floor weight, **11**. This made the car top heavy, but it didn't affect it's operation. I then added the shell to the underframe, and the cars were ready for livestock service.